THE MERCHANT OF VENICE

Wishing to court Portia, an heiress of Belmont, Bassanio asks Antonio, a Venetian merchant, for a loan. As Antonio's money is laid out in ships at sea he draws up a bond whereby Shylock, a Jew, lends 3,000 ducats for three months, with Antonio as surety. Shylock jests that Antonio must forfeit a pound of flesh if he defaults. Shylock's servant Launcelot, leaving him to serve Bassanio, takes a letter from Shylock's daughter Jessica to Lorenzo, with whom she plans to elope. Shylock, invited out to supper, gives Jessica his keys, warning her to lock all doors. Dressed as a boy she joins Lorenzo, bolting with a casket of jewels. Rumours spread of her extravagance and that Antonio's ships are lost. Bassanio sails with Gratiano to Belmont. To win Portia's hand her suitors must choose a casket containing her picture. Two princes wrongly choose gold and silver, but Bassanio correctly chooses the lead casket. His marriage with Portia takes place at once, Gratiano marrying her maid Nerissa. Lorenzo brings news that Antonio's ships are lost and that Shylock is pressing him for his bond. Bassanio and Gratiano leave at once, while Portia seeks help from Bellario, a doctor of law. At the trial Bassanio offers twice the money due but Shylock refuses it. Portia arrives disguised as a doctor of law. She extols the quality of mercy and asks Shylock to show mercy, but he claims the forfeit in the bond. Warning Antonio to be ready Portia tells Shylock a pound of Antonio's flesh is his: but if he sheds a drop of blood his estate, and for seeking the life of a citizen, his life, are both forfeit. The Duke pardons his life, Antonio waiving his half of the estate if Shylock wills it to his daughter. In gratitude Bassanio and Gratiano give the lawyer and clerk rings their wives had given them to wear always. Back in Belmont the women ask their husbands for their rings and decry their tale that they gave them to the lawyer and the clerk. When Antonio supports their story they relent, produce the rings and reveal their parts in the trial. The play ends as Nerissa hands Shylock's deed of gift to Jessica.

WILLIAM SHAKESPEARE

THE MERCHANT OF VENICE

Complete and Unabridged

CHARNWOOD
Leicester

First Charnwood Edition
published September 1991

British Library CIP Data

Shakespeare, William *1564 – 1616*
The merchant of Venice. – Large print ed. –
Charnwood library series
I. Title
822.33

ISBN 0–7089–4501–5

Published by
F. A. Thorpe (Publishing) Ltd.
Anstey, Leicestershire
Set by Words & Graphics Ltd.
Anstey, Leicestershire
Printed and bound in Great Britain by
T. J. Press (Padstow) Ltd., Padstow, Cornwall

Preface

William Shakespeare

William Shakespeare, born in Stratford-upon-Avon, was the son of John Shakespeare, a native of Snitterfield in Warwickshire, who settled in Henley Street in Stratford, where he traded as glover and merchant. He was elected to the Common Council, rising to hold office as Chamberlain. He became alderman in 1565 and Bailiff in 1568. In 1557 John Shakespeare married Mary Arden, daughter of Robert Arden, a yeoman farmer who had died leaving Mary a house and land at Wilmcote.

John and Mary had eight children, of whom three daughters died in early childhood. William, their third child and eldest son, was born on 23rd April 1564 and baptised in Holy Trinity Church, Stratford, three days later. William's three younger brothers all died comparatively early: only Joan, a younger sister, outlived him.

John Shakespeare's fortunes evidently declined; in 1578 he mortgaged his wife's property at Wilmcote and later was unable to repay the money when it fell due. From 1576 he rarely attended Council meetings and his name was finally removed from the roll of aldermen for non-attendance 'of long time'.

William is likely to have attended Stratford Grammar School, where he would have received a grounding in the 'small Latin and less Greek' Ben Jonson credited him with. While only 18 he married Anne Hathaway, eight years his senior, the daughter of Richard Hathaway, a farmer of nearby Shottery. The marriage took place by licence from the Bishop of Worcester, dated 27th November 1582, probably to avoid delay, as Anne was already pregnant. Their first child, Susanna, born in the following year, was baptised on May 26th; and within two years twins, Hamnet and Judith, were born and were baptised on 2nd February 1585.

How William supported his family in these early years is unknown. With four younger children and a far from thriving business John Shakespeare would look to his eldest son to help in providing for their joint household. Stories told about Shakespeare during these 'lost years' between 1585 and 1592 rely largely on individuals' memories and cannot be verified. One belief is that he was 'a schoolmaster in the country'; another, that he was employed by a country attorney. The legend that he was obliged to leave Stratford after being caught deer-poaching at Charlecote by Sir Thomas Lucy persists, but is similarly unverified.

Whether Shakespeare decided to seek his fortune in London or joined one of the companies of travelling actors that visited Stratford from time to time and so migrated to the London stage, the first mention of him after the birth of his twins is a bitter attack on him by a London playwright, Robert Greene. In a pamphlet written in 1592 Greene warns his fellow playwrights of 'an upstart crow, beautified with our feathers, that with his *tiger's heart wrapped in a player's hide*' (a parody of a line in Shakespeare's *Henry VI Part 3*) 'supposes he is as well able to bombast out a blank verse as the best of you and . . . is in his own conceit the only Shake-scene in a country'. The allusions to Shakespeare are unmistakeable. Friends absolved him of the charge of plagiarism; but the attack reveals that he is already making a mark in the theatre.

In Shakespeare's time neither actors nor theatres were viewed with great favour by those in authority. Actors were obliged to belong to one of the acting companies operating under the protection of a nobleman, to avoid a charge of vagrancy under the Vagrancy Act. Shakespeare belonged to the Lord Chamberlain's Company (later The King's Men) performing before the Queen and Court when called upon. The Company were paid for plays acted at the Lord Chamberlain's behest, their main income coming from takings at performances in the theatres; in Shakespeare's case *The Theatre* in Finsbury; *The Rose* and *The Globe* on Bankside; and later *The Blackfriars Theatre*.

Theatres were considered possible sites of unrest, vice and disease. Outbreaks of plague closed the theatres frequently. When this occurred in 1593 and 1594, halting the demand for plays, Shakespeare turned his hand to poetry, publishing his two long and successful poems *Venus and Adonis* and *The Rape of Lucrece*, dedicating them both to the influential young Earl of Southampton in terms indicating growing friendship.

In 1594 Shakespeare and Richard Burbage became full members of the Company, a progression that would normally follow an apprenticeship of seven years, though records so early have not survived. Each member held a share in the ownership of the Company, acting members receiving an actor's share of the takings in addition. Plays were written for the Company on contract and the playwright paid by fee, the plays becoming the property of the Company.

Unhappily Shakespeare's growing success in the theatre was marred by family tragedy. In August 1596 his only son Hamnet, one of the twins, died aged only 11; and sadly with him the male line of the Shakespeares died out. His death must have tempered the family's pleasure in the granting of a coat-of-arms to Shakespeare's father, entitling him and his son William to be styled 'Gentleman': a sure sign John Shakespeare's fortunes had recovered, and marking a milestone in our playwright's career. Next year William, then aged 33, bought New Place, one of the largest houses in Stratford-upon-Avon; tangible proof of his increasing prosperity.

In 1597 theatres were closed by the Privy Council when a comedy *The Isle of Dogs* by Thomas Nashe and Ben Jonson, played at *The Rose* was deemed to be seditious. Jonson and two fellow actors were put in prison.

Shakespeare himself did not escape trouble. His disreputable character Falstaff was originally named Sir John Oldcastle, until Lord Cobham, whose family name was Oldcastle, objected; Shakespeare was obliged to change the name to Falstaff. His play *Richard II* was potentially more dangerous. Shakespeare's scenes leading to Richard II's deposition were thought by some to parallel the political situation of Queen Elizabeth, including the Queen herself. Friends of the Earl of Essex asked the Lord Chamberlain's Men to act *Richard II* in February 1601 on the day before the Earl's abortive uprising against the Queen, for which he was executed. The Privy Council questioned the players closely about the performance but took no action.

John Shakespeare died in 1601 and is buried in Holy Trinity churchyard. In the next few years William strengthened his ties with Stratford. In 1602 he bought a parcel of land in Old Stratford and a cottage in Chapel Lane In 1605 for the large sum of £450 he was assigned one half of all the tithes of Stratford, Old Stratford, Welcombe and Bishopton, at annual value of £60.

In 1607 Shakespeare's elder daughter Susanna married John Hall, a rising young physician who built up a substantial practice around Stratford.

Their daughter Elizabeth was born next year, shortly before the death of Shakespeare's mother Mary, who is buried with her husband.

In 1608 Richard Burbage and the Company took over *The Blackfriars Theatre* for winter use. *The Globe Theatre* was open to the air and plays were acted by daylight, whereas *The Blackfriars Theatre*, enclosed, provided more comfort for audiences and, with the use of lighting, the opportunity for more elaborate stage effects.

Shakespeare is believed to have returned to live in his native Stratford in 1610 when he was 46, although he continued his association with the theatre for some years longer. It was during a performance of his play *King Henry VIII* in 1613 when cannons were fired at the entrance of the King, that *The Globe Theatre* caught fire and was burnt to the ground, destroying, it is believed, irreplaceable records relating to Shakespeare and The Company.

In 1613 Shakespeare bought a dwelling place near the theatre in Blackfriars, the only property he is known to have bought in London. He seems never to have lived in it and to have rented it to one John Robinson. William Johnson, host of the Mermaid Tavern, John Jackson and John Heminges are named with Shakespeare, but evidently only as trustees. In his will Shakespeare left the property to his daughter Susanna.

In February 1616 Shakespeare's younger daughter, the surviving twin Judith, married

Thomas Quiney, the son of his old friend, Richard Quiney; though the revelation of young Quiney's responsibility for the pregnancy of a young woman, Mary Wheeler, clouded the occasion.

Evidently ailing, Shakespeare had given instructions for his will to be drawn up in January. Perhaps doubtful about his new son-in-law's suitability as a husband for Judith, he took steps when revising his will in March to safeguard her position, laying down that one half of her bequest would become payable only when Quiney had settled on his wife lands worth an equivalent amount. This episode and the death of his brother-in-law William Hart, husband of his sister Joan, at the house in Henley Street, may have affected Shakespeare's failing health. Hart was buried on 17th April. Shakespeare died six days later on 23rd April 1616, his 53rd birthday, and was buried on 26th April in the chancel of Holy Trinity Church. His wife survived him by seven years and is buried by his side. His gravestone bears the inscription:

Good friend for Jesus sake forbear
To dig the dust enclosed here:
Blest be the man that spares these stones,
And curst be he that moves my bones.

The popularity of Shakespeare's plays during his lifetime is apparent from the lasting success of the Company, of which he was leading playwright, his own growing prosperity, and the pleasure his plays evidently gave to the Courts of Queen Elizabeth and King James. Printed editions of some of his plays achieved large sales and several reprints.

In his choice of themes he appears to have sensed the moods of the time: the surge of interest in England's past following the defeat of the Armada; a renewed feeling of patriotic fervour and interest in wars at the time of the expedition to Ireland; the perennial enjoyment of comedy and romance; the fashion for plays in Italian settings. After the death of Elizabeth a more sombre outlook emerges; changing in the last group of plays to a mood in which alienation and conflict give way to hope and reconciliation.

The Lord Chamberlain's Company regularly acted before the Queen at Christmas-time. In *A Midsummer Night's Dream* Shakespeare paid a graceful tribute to Her Majesty. There is a tradition that the Queen so enjoyed his portrayal of Falstaff in *Henry IV Parts 1 and 2* that she commanded him to write another play showing Falstaff in love, and requiring it to be ready in a fortnight. Signs of haste in the play, *The Merry Wives of Windsor*, and allusions in the text to an impending great occasion lend colour to this story.

In 1598 Francis Meres, in his *Palladis Tamia*, praised 'mellifluous and honey-tongued Shakespeare' for his *Venus and Adonis, Lucrece* and 'sugared Sonnets', ranking his comedies (*Two Gentlemen of Verona, Comedy of Errors, Love's Labour's Lost, Midsummer Night's Dream* and *Merchant of Venice*) with those of Plautus, and his tragedies (*Richard II, Richard III, Henry IV, King John, Titus Andronicus* and *Romeo and Juliet*) with those of Seneca.

Upon the accession of King James in 1603 the Lord Chamberlain's Company was authorized to become the King's Men and to play Comedies, Tragedies, Histories, etc., within their usual house *The Globe* and elsewhere. Under King James, who took a keen interest in drama, the King's Men acted more frequently before the Court, performing several plays at Christmas-time. In 1613 *The Tempest* was played before the King for the marriage celebrations of the Princess Elizabeth.

Of the thirty-seven plays believed to be wholly or partly by Shakespeare, nineteen were published in separate quarto editions during his lifetime, *Othello* also being published in this format in 1622. After his death Shakespeare's fellow actors John Heminge, the Company's manager, and Henry Condell undertook the editing of his plays, which were published in one folio volume, The First Folio, in 1623. This volume, including seventeen plays published for the first time contains Shakespeare's complete output of plays, divided into Comedies, Histories and Tragedies; except *Pericles*, which was published in an unauthorized edition in 1609 but omitted from the First Folio.

Ben Jonson, Shakespeare's great rival and candid critic, addressed him in his poem for the First Folio as 'My Beloved, The Author William Shakespeare', writing of him:

'I confess thy writings to be such
As neither man nor muse can praise too much'

and declaring

'He was not of an age but for all time'.

Later critics, including Dryden, Dr. Johnson and Coleridge, in assessing his achievement, have ranked him among the greatest of poets and dramatists.

His appeal today probably owes much to his profound understanding of the human spirit and his ability to represent men's and women's struggles to surmount life's tribulations. His superb delineation of characters must rank among his greatest accomplishments. His foremost roles — Richard III, Macbeth, Hamlet, Falstaff, Othello, Shylock, Lear — are figures of commanding presence, with all their human frailties. Many less prominent figures have unmistakeable identities, delighting or disturbing us in their roles and their relationships with other characters. Shakespeare peopled his plays with heroes and villains; nobles and artisans; learned and simple; young and old; men and women. His soldiers and country-folk bear in their speech the certain stamp of their condition and origins.

Shakespeare's range of themes and dramatic encounters confronts us with moral issues as fresh today as in his own time. Cruelty, treachery, dishonesty and unkindness are starkly portrayed and their protagonists remitted to our judgement. Several plays treat of simple domestic conflicts and trace the uneasy course of true love. His scenes of tenderness reveal a sureness of touch rivalling his mastery of contention and battle. His wit and robust humour are seldom absent from the action even in his tragedies. The plays are written in powerful and rhythmic verse and prose, many including some of the finest passages in our language.

Shakespeare's reputation has grown with the years. His plays have been published in numerous editions, translated into many languages and acted in countries throughout the world. This edition is the first to provide readers with large print copies of his works.

K. J. Rider

From careful study of published texts, performances and associated evidence, the probable order and approximate dates of composition of Shakespeare's plays has been established. A table of his works is appended.

Approximate Dates of Composition of Shakespeare's Works

Plays

By 1592   Henry VI Part 1

By 1594   Henry VI Parts 2 and 3
           Richard III
           Titus Andronicus
           The Comedy of Errors
           Love's Labours Lost
           The Two Gentlemen of Verona
           The Taming of the Shrew

1594–1597 Romeo and Juliet
           A Midsummer Night's Dream
           Richard II
           King John
           The Merchant of Venice

1597–1600	Henry IV Parts 1 and 2
	Henry V
	Much Ado About Nothing
	The Merry Wives of Windsor
	As You Like It
	Julius Caesar
	Troilus and Cressida
1601–1603	Hamlet
	Twelfth Night
	Othello
1603–1608	Measure for Measure
	All's Well That Ends Well
	King Lear
	Macbeth
	Timon of Athens
	Antony and Cleopatra
	Coriolanus
After 1608	Pericles (omitted from the Folio)
	Cymbeline
	The Winter's Tale
	The Tempest
1613	Henry VIII

Poems

1593   Venus and Adonis

1594   The Rape of Lucrece

1593–1600   The Sonnets (Published 1609)

1601   The Phoenix and The Turtle

1609   A Lover's Complaint

THE MERCHANT OF VENICE

Characters

DUKE OF VENICE.

PRINCE OF MOROCCO,
PRINCE OF ARRAGON,
$\Big\}$ suitors to Portia.

ANTONIO, a merchant of Venice.

BASSANIO, his kinsman and friend.

SOLANIO,
SALARINO,
GRATIANO,
$\Big\}$ friends to Antonio and Bassanio.

LORENZO, in love with Jessica.

SHYLOCK, a rich Jew.

TUBAL, a Jew, his friend.

LAUNCELOT GOBBO, a clown, servant to Shylock.

OLD GOBBO, father to Launcelot.

LEONARDO, servant to Bassanio.

BALTHAZAR,
STEPHANO,
$\Big\}$ servants to Portia.

PORTIA, a rich heiress.

NERISSA,   her waiting-maid.

JESSICA,   daughter to Shylock.

MAGNIFICOES OF VENICE, OFFICERS OF THE COURT OF JUSTICE, GAOLER, SERVANTS, and other ATTENDANTS.

SCENE — Partly at Venice, and partly at Belmont, the seat of Portia, on the Continent.

ACT I

Scene I.

Venice. A street.
Enter ANTONIO, SALARINO, *and* SOLANIO.

ANTONIO.
In sooth, I know not why I am so sad:
It wearies me; you say it wearies you;
But how I caught it, found it, or came by it,
What stuff 'tis made of, whereof it is born,
I am to learn;
And such a want-wit sadness makes of me,
That I have much ado to know myself.

SALARINO.
Your mind is tossing on the ocean;
There, where your argosies with portly sail, —
Like signiors and rich burghers of the flood, —
Or, as it were, the pageants of the sea, —
Do overpeer the petty traffickers,
That curtsey to them, do them reverence,
As they fly by them with their woven wings.

SOLANIO.
Believe me, sir, had I such venture forth,
The better part of my affections would
Be with my hopes abroad. I should be still
Plucking the grass, to know where sits the wind;
Peering in maps for ports, and piers, and roads;

5

And every object that might make me fear
Misfortune to my ventures, out of doubt
Would make me sad.
SALARINO.

        My wind, cooling my broth,
Would blow me to an ague, when I thought
What harm a wind too great might do at sea.
I should not see the sandy hour-glass run,
But I should think of shallows and of flats;
And see my wealthy Andrew dock'd in sand,
Vailing her high-top lower than her ribs,
To kiss her burial. Should I go to church,
And see the holy edifice of stone,
And not bethink me straight of dangerous
rocks,
Which touching but my gentle vessel's side,
Would scatter all her spices on the stream;
Enrobe the roaring waters with my silks;
And, in a word, but even now worth this,
And now worth nothing? Shall I have the
thought
To think on this; and shall I lack the thought,
That such a thing bechanced would make me
sad?
But tell not me; I know Antonio
Is sad to think upon his merchandise.
ANTONIO.

Believe me, no: I thank my fortune for it,
My ventures are not in one bottom trusted,
Nor to one place; nor is my whole estate
Upon the fortune of this present year:
Therefore my merchandise makes me not sad.

SALARINO.
Why, then you are in love.
ANTONIO.
                                            Fie, fie!
SALARINO.
Not in love neither? Then let's say you're sad,
Because you are not merry: and 'twere as easy
For you to laugh, and leap, and say you are
merry,
Because you are not sad. Now, by two-headed
Janus,
Nature hath framed strange fellows in her
time:
Some that will evermore peep through their
eyes,
And laugh, like parrots, at a bag-piper;
And other of such vinegar aspect,
That they'll not show their teeth in way
of smile,
Though Nestor swear the jest be laughable.
SOLANIO.
Here comes Bassanio, your most noble kinsman,
Gratiano, and Lorenzo. Fare ye well:
We leave you now with better company.
SALARINO.
I would have stay'd till I had made you merry,
If worthier friends had not prevented me.
ANTONIO.
Your worth is very dear in my regard.
I take it, your own business calls on you,
And you embrace th' occasion to depart.

Enter BASSANIO, LORENZO, *and* GRATIANO.

SALARINO.
Good morrow, my good lords.
BASSANIO.
Good signiors both, when shall we laugh? say,
when?
You grow exceeding strange: must it be so?
SALARINO.
We'll make our leisures to attend on yours.
                        [*Exeunt* SALARINO *and* SOLANIO.
LORENZO.
My Lord Bassanio, since you have found
Antonio,
We two will leave you: but, at dinner-time,
I pray you, have in mind where we must meet.
BASSANIO.
I will not fail you.
GRATIANO.
You look not well, Signior Antonio;
You have too much respect upon the world:
They lose it that do buy it with much care:
Believe me, you are marvellously changed.
ANTONIO.
I hold the world but as the world, Gratiano;
A stage, where every man must play a part,
And mine a sad one.
GRATIANO.
                        Let me play the fool:
With mirth and laughter let old wrinkles come;
And let my liver rather heat with wine
Than my heart cool with mortifying groans.

8

Why should a man, whose blood is warm
within,
Sit like his grandsire cut in alabaster?
Sleep when he wakes? and creep into the
jaundice
By being peevish? I tell thee what, Antonio, —
I love thee, and it is my love that speaks, —
There are a sort of men, whose visages
Do cream and mantle like a standing pond;
And do a wilful stillness entertain
With purpose to be drest in an opinion
Of wisdom, gravity, profound conceit;
As who should say, 'I am Sir Oracle,
And when I ope my lips, let no dog bark!'
O my Antonio, I do know of these,
That therefore only are reputed wise
For saying nothing; when, I am very sure,
If they should speak, would almost damn those
ears,
Which, hearing them, would call their brothers
fools.
I'll tell thee more of this another time:
But fish not, with this melancholy bait,
For this fool-gudgeon, this opinion. —
Come, good Lorenzo. — Fare ye well awhile:
I'll end my exhortation after dinner.

LORENZO.
Well, we will leave you, then, till dinner-time:
I must be one of these same dumb wise men,
For Gratiano never lets me speak.

GRATIANO.
Well, keep me company but two years moe,

9

Thou shalt not know the sound of thine own
tongue.

ANTONIO.

Farewell: I'll grow a talker for this gear.

GRATIANO.

Thanks, i'faith; for silence is only commendable
In a neat's tongue dried, and a maid not
vendible.

                              [*Exeunt* GRATIANO *and* LORENZO.

ANTONIO.

Is that any thing now?

BASSANIO.

Gratiano speaks an infinite deal of nothing,
more than any man in all Venice. His reasons
are as two grains of wheat hid in two bushels
of chaff: you shall seek all day ere you find
them; and when you have them, they are not
worth the search.

ANTONIO.

Well; tell me now, what lady is the same
To whom you swore a secret pilgrimage,
That you today promised to tell me of?

BASSANIO.

'Tis not unknown to you, Antonio,
How much I have disabled mine estate,
By something showing a more swelling port
Than my faint means would grant continuance:
Nor do I now make moan to be abridged
From such a noble rate; but my chief care
Is, to come fairly off from the great debts,
Wherein my time, something too prodigal,
Hath left me gaged. To you, Antonio,

I owe the most, in money and in love;
And from your love I have a warranty
To unburden all my plots and purposes
How to get clear of all the debts I owe.
ANTONIO.
    I pray you, good Bassanio, let me know it;
And if it stand, as you yourself still do,
Within the eye of honour, be assured
My purse, my person, my extremest means,
Lie all unlock'd to your occasions.
BASSANIO.
    In my school-days, when I had lost one shaft,
I shot his fellow of the selfsame flight
The selfsame way with more advised watch,
To find the other forth; and by advent'ring
both,
I oft found both: I urge this childhood proof,
Because what follows is pure innocence.
I owe you much; and, like a wilful youth,
That which I owe is lost: but if you please
To shoot another arrow that self way
Which you did shoot the first, I do not doubt,
As I will watch the aim, or to find both,
Or bring your latter hazard back again,
And thankfully rest debtor for the first.
ANTONIO.
    You know me well; and herein spend but time
To wind about my love with circumstance;
And out of doubt you do me now more wrong
In making question of my uttermost,
Than if you had made waste of all I have:
Then do but say to me what I should do,

That in your knowledge may by me be done,
And I am press'd unto it: therefore, speak.
BASSANIO.
In Belmont is a lady richly left;
And she is fair, and, fairer than that word,
Of wondrous virtues: sometimes from her eyes
I did receive fair speechless messages:
Her name is Portia; nothing undervalued
To Cato's daughter, Brutus' Portia:
Nor is the wide world ignorant of her worth;
For the four winds blow in from every coast
Renowned suitors: and her sunny locks
Hang on her temples like a golden fleece;
Which makes her seat of Belmont Colchos'
strond,
And many Jasons come in quest of her.
O my Antonio, had I but the means
To hold a rival place with one of them,
I have a mind presages me such thrift,
That I should questionless be fortunate!
ANTONIO.
Thou know'st that all my fortunes are at sea;
Neither have I money, nor commodity
To raise a present sum: therefore, go forth;
Try what my credit can in Venice do:
That shall be rack'd, even to the uttermost,
To furnish thee to Belmont, to fair Portia.
Go, presently inquire, and so will I,
Where money is; and I no question make,
To have it of my trust, or for my sake.

                                    [*Exeunt.*

Scene II.

PORTIA.

By my troth, Nerissa, my little body is aweary of this great world.

NERISSA.

You would be, sweet madam, if your miseries were in the same abundance as your good fortunes are: and yet, for aught I see, they are as sick that surfeit with too much, as they that starve with nothing. It is no mean happiness, therefore, to be seated in the mean: superfluity comes sooner by white hairs; but competency lives longer.

PORTIA.

Good sentences, and well pronounced.

NERISSA.

They would be better, if well follow'd.

PORTIA.

If to do were as easy as to know what were good to do, chapels had been churches, and poor men's cottages princes' palaces. It is a good divine that follows his own instructions: I can easier teach twenty what were good to be done, than be one of the twenty to follow mine

13

own teaching. The brain may devise laws for the blood; but a hot temper leaps o'er a cold decree: such a hare is madness the youth, to skip o'er the meshes of good-counsel the cripple. But this reasoning is not in the fashion to choose me a husband: — O me, the word 'choose'! I may neither choose who I would, nor refuse who I dislike; so is the will of a living daughter curb'd by the will of a dead father. — Is it not hard, Nerissa, that I cannot choose one, nor refuse none?

NERISSA.

Your father was ever virtuous; and holy men, at their death, have good inspirations: therefore, the lottery, that he hath devised in these three chests of gold, silver, and lead, — whereof who chooses his meaning chooses you, — will, no doubt, never be chosen by any rightly, but one who shall rightly love. But what warmth is there in your affection towards any of these princely suitors that are already come?

PORTIA.

I pray thee, over-name them; and as thou namest them, I will describe them; and, according to my description, level at my affection.

NERISSA.

First, there is the Neapolitan prince.

PORTIA.

Ay, that's a colt indeed, for he doth nothing but talk of his horse; and he makes it a great appropriation to his own good parts, that he can shoe him himself. I am much afeard my lady his mother play'd false with a smith.

NERISSA.

Then there is the County Palatine.

PORTIA.

He doth nothing but frown; as who should say, 'An you will not have me, choose:' he hears merry tales, and smiles not: I fear he will prove the weeping philosopher when he grows old, being so full of unmannerly sadness in his youth. I had rather be married to a Death's-head with a bone in his mouth than to either of these: — God defend me from these two!

NERISSA.

How say you by the French lord, Monsieur Le Bon?

PORTIA.

God made him, and therefore let him pass for a man. In truth, I know it is a sin to be a mocker: but, he! — why, he hath a horse better than the Neapolitan's; a better bad habit of frowning than the Count Palatine: he is every man in no man; if a throstle sing, he falls straight a-capering; he will fence with his own shadow: if I should marry him, I should marry twenty husbands. If he would despise me, I would forgive him; for if he love me to madness, I shall never requite him.

NERISSA.

What say you, then to Falconbridge, the young baron of England?

PORTIA.

You know I say nothing to him: for he

15

understands not me, nor I him: he hath neither Latin, French, nor Italian; and you will come into the court and swear that I have a poor pennyworth in the English. He is a proper man's picture; but alas, who can converse with a dumb-show? How oddly he is suited! I think he bought his doublet in Italy, his round hose in France, his bonnet in Germany, and his behaviour every where.

NERISSA.

What think you of the Scottish lord, his neighbour?

PORTIA.

That he hath a neighbourly charity in him; for he borrow'd a box of the ear of the Englishman, and swore he would pay him again when he was able: I think the Frenchman became his surety, and seal'd under for another.

NERISSA.

How like you the young German, the Duke of Saxony's nephew?

PORTIA.

Very vilely in the morning, when he is sober; and most vilely in the afternoon, when he is drunk: when he is best, he is a little worse than a man; and when he is worst, he is little better than a beast. An the worst fall that ever fell, I hope I shall make shift to go without him.

NERISSA.

If he should offer to choose, and choose the right casket, you should refuse to perform your father's will, if you should refuse to accept him.

PORTIA.

Therefore, for fear of the worst, I pray thee, set a deep glass of Rhenish wine on the contrary casket; for, if the devil be within, and that temptation without, I know he will choose it. I will do any thing, Nerissa, ere I will be married to a sponge.

NERISSA.

You need not fear, lady, the having any of these lords: they have acquainted me with their determinations; which is, indeed, to return to their home, and to trouble you with no more suit, unless you may be won by some other sort than your father's imposition, depending on the caskets.

PORTIA.

If I live to be as old as Sibylla, I will die as chaste as Diana, unless I be obtain'd by the manner of my father's will. I am glad this parcel of wooers are so reasonable; for there is not one among them but I dote on his very absence; and I pray God grant them a fair departure.

NERISSA.

Do you not remember, lady, in your father's time, a Venetian, a scholar and a soldier, that came hither in company of the Marquis of Montferrat?

PORTIA.

Yes, yes, it was Bassanio: as I think, so was he call'd.

NERISSA.

True, madam: he, of all the men that ever my foolish eyes look'd upon, was the best deserving a fair lady.

PORTIA.

I remember him well; and I remember him worthy of thy praise.

Enter a SERVANT.

How now! what news?

SERVANT.

The four strangers seek for you, madam, to take their leave: and there is a forerunner come from a fifth, the Prince of Morocco; who brings word, the prince his master will be here tonight.

PORTIA.

If a could bid the fifth welcome with so good a heart as I can bid the other four farewell, I should be glad of his approach: if he have the condition of a saint and the complexion of a devil, I had rather he should shrive me than wive me.

Come, Nerissa. — Sirrah, go before. —

Whiles we shut the gates upon one wooer, another knocks at the door.

[*Exeunt.*

Scene III.

Venice. A public place.
Enter BASSANIO *with* SHYLOCK *the Jew.*

SHYLOCK.
  Three thousand ducats, — well.
BASSANIO.
  Ay, sir, for three months.
SHYLOCK.
  For three months, — well.
BASSANIO.
  For the which, as I told you, Antonio shall be
  bound.
SHYLOCK.
  Antonio shall become bound, — well.
BASSANIO.
  May you stead me? will you pleasure me? shall
  I know your answer?
SHYLOCK.
  Three thousand ducats for three months, and
  Antonio bound.
BASSANIO.
  Your answer to that.
SHYLOCK.
  Antonio is a good man.
BASSANIO.
  Have you heard any imputation to the contrary?

19

SHYLOCK.

Ho, no, no, no, no; — my meaning, in saying he is a good man is to have you understand me that he is sufficient. Yet his means are in supposition: he hath an argosy bound to Tripolis, another to the Indies; I understand, moreover, upon the Rialto, he hath a third at Mexico, a fourth for England, — and other ventures he hath, squander'd abroad. But ships are but boards, sailors but men: there be land-rats and water-rats, water-thieves and land-thieves, I mean pirates; and then there is the peril of waters, winds, and rocks. The man is, notwithstanding, sufficient: — three thousand ducats: — I think I may take his bond.

BASSANIO.

Be assured you may.

SHYLOCK.

I will be assured I may; and, that I may be assured, I will bethink me. May I speak with Antonio?

BASSANIO.

If it please you to dine with us.

SHYLOCK.

Yes, to smell pork; to eat of the habitation which your prophet the Nazarite conjured the devil into. I will buy with you, sell with you, talk with you, walk with you, and so following; but I will not eat with you, drink with you, nor pray with you. What news on the Rialto? — Who is he comes here?

Enter ANTONIO.

BASSANIO.
This is Signior Antonio.
SHYLOCK [*aside*].
How like a fawning publican he looks!
I hate him for he is a Christian!
But more, for that, in low simplicity,
He lends out money gratis, and brings down
The rate of usance here with us in Venice.
If I can catch him once upon the hip,
I will feed fat the ancient grudge I bear him.
He hates our sacred nation; and he rails,
Even there where merchants most do congregate,
On me, my bargains, and my well-won thrift,
Which he calls interest. Cursed be my tribe,
If I forgive him!
BASSANIO.
                         Shylock, do you hear?
SHYLOCK.
I am debating of my present store;
And, by the near guess of my memory,
I cannot instantly raise up the gross
Of full three thousand ducats. What of that?
Tubal, a wealthy Hebrew of my tribe,
Will furnish me. But soft! how many months
Do you desire? — Rest you fair, good signior;
                                        [*to* ANTONIO.
Your worship was the last man in our mouths.
ANTONIO.
Shylock, although I neither lend nor borrow
By taking nor by giving of excess,

21

Yet, to supply the ripe wants of my friend,
I'll break a custom. — Is he yet possess'd
How much ye would?

SHYLOCK.

              Ay, ay, three thousand ducats.

ANTONIO.

And for three months.

SHYLOCK.

I had forgot, — three months, you told me so.
Well, then, your bond; and let me see, — but
hear you;
Methought you said you neither lend nor
borrow
Upon advantage.

ANTONIO.

              I do never use it.

SHYLOCK.

When Jacob grazed his uncle Laban's sheep, —
This Jacob from our holy Abram was
(As his wise mother wrought in his behalf)
The third possessor; ay, he was the third, —

ANTONIO.

And what of him? did he take interest?

SHYLOCK.

No, not take interest; not as you would say,
Directly interest: mark what Jacob did.
When Laban and himself were compromised
That all the eanlings which were streak'd and
pied
Should fall as Jacob's hire, the ewes, being
rank,
In th'end of autumn turned to the rams;

And when the work of generation was
Between these woolly breeders in the act,
The skilful shepherd peel'd me certain wands,
And, in the doing of the deed of kind,
He stuck them up before the fulsome ewes,
Who, then conceiving, did in eaning time
Fall parti-colour'd lambs, and those were Jacob's.
This was a way to thrive, and he was blest:
And thrift is blessing, if men steal it not.

ANTONIO.

This was a venture, sir, that Jacob served for;
A thing not in his power to bring to pass,
But sway'd and fashion'd by the hand of
heaven.
Was this inserted to make interest good?
Or is your gold and silver ewes and rams?

SHYLOCK.

I cannot tell: I make it breed as fast: —
But note me, signior.

ANTONIO.

                              Mark you this, Bassanio,
The devil can cite Scripture for his purpose.
An evil soul, producing holy witness,
Is like a villain with a smiling cheek;
A goodly apple rotten at the heart:
O, what a goodly outside falsehood hath!

SHYLOCK.

Three thousand ducats, — 'tis a good round
sum.
Three months from twelve, — then, let me see,
the rate —

ANTONIO.
　Well, Shylock, shall we be beholden to you?
SHYLOCK.
　Signior Antonio, many a time and oft,
　In the Rialto, you have rated me
　About my moneys and my usances:
　Still have I borne it with a patient shrug;
　For sufferance is the badge of all our tribe:
　You call me misbeliever, cut-throat dog,
　And spit upon my Jewish gaberdine,
　And all for use of that which is mine own.
　Well, then, it now appears you need my help:
　Go to, then; you come to me, and you say,
　'Shylock, we would have moneys:' — you say
　so;
　You, that did void your rheum upon my beard,
　And foot me as you spurn a stranger cur
　Over your threshold: moneys is your suit.
　What should I say to you? Should I not say,
　'Hath a dog money? is it possible
　A cur can lend three thousand ducats?' or
　Shall I bend low, and in a bondman's key,
　With bated breath and whispering humbleness,
　Say this, —
　'Fair sir, you spit on me on Wednesday last;
　You spurn'd me such a day; another time
　You call'd me dog; and for these courtesies
　I'll lend you thus much moneys'?
ANTONIO.
　I am as like to call thee so again,
　To spit on thee again, to spurn thee too.
　If thou wilt lend this money, lend it not

As to thy friends — for when did friendship take
A breed for barren metal of his friend? —
But lend it rather to thine enemy;
Who if he break, thou mayst with better face
Exact the penalty.

SHYLOCK.
                        Why, look you, how you storm!
I would be friends with you, and have your love,
Forget the shames that you have stain'd me with,
Supply your present wants, and take no doit
Of usance for my moneys,
And you'll not hear me: this is kind I offer.

BASSANIO.
This were kindness.

SHYLOCK.
                        This kindness will I show: —
Go with me to a notary, seal me there
Your single bond; and, in a merry sport,
If you repay me not on such a day,
In such a place, such sum or sums as are
Express'd in the condition, let the forfeit
Be nominated for an equal pound
Of your fair flesh, to be cut off and taken
In what part of your body pleaseth me.

ANTONIO.
Content, i'faith: I'll seal to such a bond,
And say there is much kindness in the Jew.

BASSANIO.
You shall not seal to such a bond for me:

I'll rather dwell in my necessity.

ANTONIO.

Why, fear not, man; I will not forfeit it:
Within these two months, that's a month
before
This bond expires, I do expect return
Of thrice three times the value of this bond.

SHYLOCK.

O father Abram, what these Christians are,
Whose own hard dealings teaches them suspect
The thoughts of others! — Pray you, tell me
this;
If he should break his day, what should I gain
By the exaction of the forfeiture?
A pound of man's flesh taken from a man
Is not so estimable, profitable neither,
As flesh of muttons, beefs, or goats. I say,
To buy his favour, I extend this friendship:
If he will take it, so; if not, adieu;
And, for my love, I pray you wrong me not.

ANTONIO.

Yes, Shylock, I will seal unto this bond.

SHYLOCK.

Then meet me forthwith at the notary's, —
Give him direction for this merry bond;
And I will go and purse the ducats straight;
See to my house, left in the fearful guard
Of an unthrifty knave; and presently
I will be with you.

ANTONIO.

Hie thee, gentle Jew.

[*Exit* SHYLOCK.

26

The Hebrew will turn Christian: he grows
kind.
BASSANIO.
I like not fair terms and a villain's mind.
ANTONIO.
Come on: in this there can be no dismay;
My ships come home a month before the day.
                                    [*Exeunt.*

ACT II

Scene I.

Belmont. A room in PORTIA'S house.
Enter the PRINCE OF MOROCCO, *a tawny Moor all in white, and three or four* FOLLOWERS *accordingly, with* PORTIA, NERISSA, *and their* TRAIN. *Flourish of cornets.*

PRINCE OF MOROCCO.
Mislike me not for my complexion,
The shadow'd livery of the burnish'd sun,
To whom I am a neighbour and near bred.
Bring me the fairest creature northward born,
Where Phoebus' fire scarce thaws the icicles,
And let us make incision for your love,
To prove whose blood is reddest, his or mine.
I tell thee, lady, this aspect of mine
Hath fear'd the valiant: by my love, I swear
The best-regarded virgins of our clime
Hath loved it too: I would not change this hue,
Except to steal your thoughts, my gentle queen.
PORTIA.
In terms of choice I am not solely led
By nice direction of a maiden's eyes;
Besides, the lottery of my destiny
Bars me the right of voluntary choosing:

31

But, if my father had not scanted me,
And hedg'd me by his will, to yield myself
His wife who wins me by that means I told
you,
Yourself, renowned prince, then stood as fair
As any comer I have look'd on yet
For my affection.

PRINCE OF MOROCCO.
                    Even for that I thank you:
Therefore, I pray you, lead me to the caskets,
To try my fortune. By this scimitar,
That slew the Sophy and a Persian prince
That won three fields of Sultan Solyman,
I would outstare the sternest eyes that look,
Outbrave the heart most daring on the earth,
Pluck the young sucking-cubs from the she-
bear,
Yea, mock the lion when he roars for prey,
To win thee, lady. But, alas the while!
If Hercules and Lichas play at dice
Which is the better man, the greater throw
May turn by fortune from the weaker hand:
So is Alcides beaten by his page;
And so may I, blind Fortune leading me,
Miss that which one unworthier may attain,
And die with grieving.

PORTIA.
                    You must take your chance;
And either not attempt to choose at all,
Or swear before you choose, — if you choose
wrong,
Never to speak to lady afterward

In way of marriage: therefore be advised.
PRINCE OF MOROCCO.
Nor will not. Come, bring me unto my chance.
PORTIA.
First, forward to the temple: after dinner
Your hazard shall be made.
PRINCE OF MOROCCO.
                                        Good fortune, then!
To make me blest or cursed'st among men.
                                        [*Cornets, and exeunt.*

Scene II.

Venice. A street.
Enter LAUNCELOT *the Clown, alone.*

LAUNCELOT GOBBO.

Certainly my conscience will serve me to run from this Jew my master. The fiend is at mine elbow, and tempts me, saying to me, 'Gobbo, Launcelot Gobbo, good Launcelot,' or 'good Gobbo,' or 'good Launcelot Gobbo, use your legs, take the start, run away.' My conscience says, 'No; take heed, honest Launcelot; take heed, honest Gobbo,' or, as aforesaid, 'honest Launcelot Gobbo; do not run; scorn running with thy heels.' Well, the most courageous fiend bids me pack: '*Via!*' says the fiend, 'away!' says the fiend; 'for the heavens, rouse up a brave mind,' says the fiend, 'and run.' Well, my conscience, hanging about the neck of my heart, says very wisely to me, 'My honest friend Launcelot, being an honest man's son,' – or rather an honest woman's son; – for, indeed, my father did something smack, something grow to, – he had a kind of taste; – well, my conscience says, 'Launcelot, budge not.' 'Budge,' says the fiend. 'Budge not,' says my conscience. 'Conscience,' say I, 'you counsel well; 'fiend,' say I, 'you counsel well:' to be ruled by my conscience, I should stay with the Jew my master, who — God bless the mark! — is a kind of devil; and, to run away from the Jew, I should be ruled by the fiend, who, saving your reverence, is the devil himself. Certainly the Jew is the very devil incarnal; and, in my conscience, my conscience is but a kind of hard conscience, to offer to counsel me to stay with the Jew. The fiend gives the more friendly counsel: I will run, fiend; my heels are at your command; I will run.

Enter OLD GOBBO, *with a basket.*

OLD GOBBO.
Master young man, you, I pray you, which is the way to master Jew's?
LAUNCELOT GOBBO [*aside*].
O heavens, this is my true-begotten father! who, being more than sand-blind, high-gravel-blind, knows me not: — I will try confusions with him.
OLD GOBBO.
Master young gentleman, I pray you, which is the way to master Jew's?
LAUNCELOT GOBBO.
Turn up on your right hand at the next turning, but, at the next turning of all, on your left; marry, at the very next turning, turn of no hand, but turn down indirectly to the Jew's house.

OLD GOBBO.

By God's sonties, 'twill be a hard way to hit. Can you tell me whether one Launcelot, that dwells with him, dwell with him or no?

LAUNCELOT GOBBO.

Talk you of young Master Launcelot? —
                                            [*aside*]
Mark me now; now will I raise the waters. — Talk you of young Master Launcelot?

OLD GOBBO.

No master, sir, but a poor man's son: his father, though I say it, is an honest exceeding poor man, and, God be thank'd, well to live.

LAUNCELOT GOBBO.

Well, let his father be what a' will, we talk of young Master Launcelot.

OLD GOBBO.

Your worship's friend, and Launcelot, sir.

LAUNCELOT GOBBO.

But, I pray you, *ergo*, old man, *ergo*, I beseech you, talk you of young Master Launcelot?

OLD GOBBO.

Of Launcelot, an't please your mastership.

LAUNCELOT GOBBO.

Ergo, Master Launcelot. Talk not of Master Launcelot, father; for the young gentleman — according to Fates and Destinies, and such odd sayings, the Sisters Three, and such branches of learning — is, indeed, deceased; or, as you would say in plain terms, gone to heaven.

OLD GOBBO.

Marry, God forbid! the boy was the very staff

of my age, my very prop.

LAUNCELOT GOBBO.

Do I look like a cudgel or a hovel-post, a staff,
or a prop? — Do you know me, father?

OLD GOBBO.

Alack the day, I know you not, young gentleman:
but, I pray you, tell me, is my boy — God rest
his soul! — alive or dead?

LAUNCELOT GOBBO.

Do you not know me, father?

OLD GOBBO.

Alack, sir, I am sand-blind; I know you not.

LAUNCELOT GOBBO.

Nay, indeed, if you had your eyes, you might
fail of the knowing me: it is a wise father that
knows his own child. Well, old man, I will tell
you news of your son: give me your blessing
                                          [*kneels*]:
truth will come to light; murder cannot be hid
long, — a man's son may; but, in the end, truth
will out.

OLD GOBBO.

Pray you, sir, stand up: I am sure you are not
Launcelot, my boy.

LAUNCELOT GOBBO.

Pray you, let's have no more fooling about it,
but give me your blessing: I am Launcelot,
your boy that was, your son that is, your child
that shall be.

OLD GOBBO.

I cannot think you are my son.

LAUNCELOT GOBBO.

I know not what I shall think of that: but I am Launcelot, the Jew's man; and I am sure Margery your wife is my mother.

OLD GOBBO.

Her name is Margery, indeed: I'll be sworn, if thou be Launcelot, thou art mine own flesh and blood. Lord worshipp'd might he be! what a beard hast thou got! thou hast got more hair on thy chin than Dobbin my fill-horse has on his tail.

LAUNCELOT GOBBO [*rising*].

It should seem, then, that Dobbin's tail grows backward; I am sure he had more hair of his tail than I have of my face when I last saw him.

OLD GOBBO.

Lord, how art thou changed! How dost thou and thy master agree? I have brought him a present. How 'gree you now?

LAUNCELOT GOBBO.

Well, well: but, for mine own part, as I have set up my rest to run away, so I will not rest till I have run some ground. My master's a very Jew: give him a present! give him a halter: I am famish'd in his service; you may tell every finger I have with my ribs. Father, I am glad you are come: give me your present to one Master Bassanio, who, indeed, gives rare new liveries: if I serve not him, I will run as far as God has any ground. — O rare fortune! here comes the man: — to him, father; for I am a Jew, if I serve the Jew any longer.

39

Enter BASSANIO, *with* LEONARDO *and a*
FOLLOWER *or two.*

BASSANIO.

You may do so; — but let it be so hasted, that
supper be ready at the furthest by five of the
clock. See these letters deliver'd; put the liveries
to making; and desire Gratiano to come anon to
my lodging.

[*Exit a* SERVANT.

LAUNCELOT GOBBO.

To him, father.

OLD GOBBO.

God bless your worship!

BASSANIO.

Gramercy: wouldst thou aught with me?

OLD GOBBO.

Here's my son, sir, a poor boy, —

LAUNCELOT GOBBO.

Not a poor boy, sir, but the rich Jew's man; that
would, sir, — as my father shall specify, —

OLD GOBBO.

He hath a great infection, sir, as one would say,
to serve, —

LAUNCELOT GOBBO.

Indeed, the short and the long is, I serve the
Jew, and have a desire, — as my father shall
specify, —

OLD GOBBO.

His master and he — saving your worship's
reverence — are scarce cater-cousins, —

LAUNCELOT GOBBO.

To be brief, the very truth is, that the Jew having done me wrong, doth cause me, — as my father, being, I hope, an old man, shall frutify unto you, —

OLD GOBBO.

I have here a dish of doves that I would bestow upon your worship; and my suit is, —

LAUNCELOT GOBBO.

In very brief, the suit is impertinent to myself, as your worship shall know by this honest old man; and, though I say it, though old man, yet poor man, my father.

BASSANIO.

One speak for both. — What would you?

LAUNCELOT GOBBO.

Serve you, sir.

OLD GOBBO.

That is the very defect of the matter, sir.

BASSANIO.

I know thee well; thou hast obtain'd thy suit:
Shylock thy master spoke with me this day,
And hath preferr'd thee, — if it be preferment
To leave a rich Jew's service, to become
The follower of so poor a gentleman.

LAUNCELOT GOBBO.

The old proverb is very well parted between my master Shylock and you, sir: you have the grace of God, sir, and he hath enough.

BASSANIO.

Thou speak'st it well. — Go, father, with thy son. —

Take leave of thy old master, and inquire
My lodging out. — Give him a livery
More guarded than his fellows': see it done.

LAUNCELOT GOBBO.

Father, in. — I cannot get a service, no; — I
have ne'er a tongue in my head — Well
                    [*looking on his palm*],
if any man in Italy have a fairer table, which
doth offer to swear upon a book, I shall have
good fortune! — Go to, here's a simple line of
life! here's a small trifle of wives! alas, fifteen
wives is nothing! eleven widows and nine maids
is a simple coming-in for one man; and then to
scape drowning thrice, and to be in peril of my
life with the edge of a feather-bed, — here are
simple scapes! Well, if Fortune be a woman,
she's a good wench for this gear. — Father,
come; I'll take my leave of the Jew in the
twinkling of an eye.
            [*Exeunt* LAUNCELOT *and* OLD GOBBO.

BASSANIO.

I pray thee, good Leonardo, think on this:
These things being bought and orderly bestow'd,
Return in haste, for I do feast tonight
My best-esteem'd acquaintance: hie thee, go.

LEONARDO.

My best endeavours shall be done herein.

Enter GRATIANO.

GRATIANO.

Where's your master?

42

LEONARDO.
> Yonder, sir, he walks.
>> [*Exit.*

GRATIANO.
Signior Bassanio, —

BASSANIO.
Gratiano!

GRATIANO.
I have a suit to you.

BASSANIO.
> You have obtain'd it.

GRATIANO.
You must not deny me: I must go with you
to Belmont.

BASSANIO.
Why, then you must. But hear thee, Gratiano:
Thou art too wild, too rude, and bold of
voice, —
Parts that become thee happily enough,
And in such eyes as ours appear not faults;
But where thou art not known, why, there they
show
Something too liberal. Prithee, take pain
To allay with some cold drops of modesty
Thy skipping spirit; lest, through thy wild
behaviour,
I be misconstred in the place I go to,
And lose my hopes.

GRATIANO.
> Signior Bassanio, hear me:
If I do not put on a sober habit,
Talk with respect, and swear but now and then,

TMOV5

Wear prayer-books in my pocket, look demurely;
Nay, more, while grace is saying, hood mine
eyes
Thus with my hat, and sigh, and say amen;
Use all the observance of civility,
Like one well studied in a sad ostent
To please his grandam, — never trust me
more.

BASSANIO.

Well, we shall see your bearing.

GRATIANO.

Nay, but I bar tonight: you shall not gauge me
By what we do tonight.

BASSANIO.

                              No, that were pity:
I would entreat you rather to put on
Your boldest suit of mirth, for we have friends
That purpose merriment. But fare ye well:
I have some business.

GRATIANO.

And I must to Lorenzo and the rest:
But we will visit you at supper-time.

                                   [*Exeunt.*

Scene III.

The same. A room in SHYLOCK'S house.
Enter JESSICA AND LAUNCELOT.

JESSICA.
I am sorry thou wilt leave my father so:
Our house is hell: and thou, a merry devil,
Didst rob it of some taste of tediousness.
But fare thee well; there is a ducat for thee:
And, Launcelot, soon at supper shalt thou see
Lorenzo, who is thy new master's guest:
Give him this letter; do it secretly; —
And so farewell: I would not have my father
See me in talk with thee.

LAUNCELOT GOBBO.
Adieu; tears exhibit my tongue. Most beautiful
pagan, most sweet Jew! if a Christian did not
play the knave and get thee, I am much
deceived. But, adieu: these foolish drops do
something drown my manly spirit: adieu.

JESSICA.
Farewell, good Launcelot. —

[*Exit* LAUNCELOT.
Alack, what heinous sin is it in me
To be ashamed to be my father's child!
But though I am a daughter to his blood,
I am not to his manners. O Lorenzo,

45

If thou keep promise, I shall end this strife, —
Become a Christian, and thy loving wife!
                                        [*Exit.*

Scene IV.

The same. A street.
Enter GRATIANO, LORENZO, SALARINO, *and*
SOLANIO.

LORENZO.
Nay, we will slink away in supper-time,
Disguise us at my lodging, and return
All in an hour.

GRATIANO.
We have not made good preparation.

SALARINO.
We have not spoke us yet of torch-bearers.

SOLANIO.
'Tis vile, unless it may be quaintly order'd,
And better in my mind not undertook.

LORENZO.
'Tis now but four o'clock: we have two hours
To furnish us.

Enter LAUNCELOT, *with a letter.*

Friend Launcelot, what's the news?

LAUNCELOT GOBBO.
An it shall please you to break up this, it shall
seem to signify.

47

LORENZO.

I know the hand: in faith, 'tis a fair hand;
And whiter than the paper it writ on
Is the fair hand that writ.

GRATIANO.

Love-news, in faith.

LAUNCELOT GOBBO.

By your leave, sir.

LORENZO.

Whither goest thou?

LAUNCELOT GOBBO.

Marry, sir, to bid my old master the Jew to
sup tonight with my new master the Christian.

LORENZO.

Hold here, take this

[*gives money*]:
— tell gentle Jessica
I will not fail her; speak it privately; go. —

[*Exit* LAUNCELOT.

Gentlemen, will you prepare you for this mask
tonight?
I am provided of a torch-bearer.

SALARINO.

Ay, marry, I'll be gone about it straight.

SOLANIO.

And so will I.

LORENZO.

Meet me and Gratiano
At Gratiano's lodging some hour hence.

SALARINO.

'Tis good we do so.

[*Exeunt* SALARINO *and* SOLANIO.

GRATIANO.
  Was not that letter from fair Jessica?
LORENZO.
  I must needs tell thee all. She hath directed
  How I shall take her from her father's house;
  What gold and jewels she is furnish'd with;
  What page's suit she hath in readiness.
  If e'er the Jew her father come to heaven,
  It will be for his gentle daughter's sake:
  And never dare misfortune cross her foot,
  Unless she do it under this excuse, —
  That she is issue to a faithless Jew.
  Come, go with me: peruse this as thou goest:
  Fair Jessica shall be my torch-bearer.
                                   [*Exeunt.*

Scene V.

The same. Before SHYLOCK'S house.
Enter SHYLOCK *and* LAUNCELOT.

SHYLOCK.
   Well, thou shalt see, thy eyes shall be thy judge,
   The difference of old Shylock and Bassanio: —
   What, Jessica! — thou shalt not gormandize,
   As thou has done with me; — what, Jessica! —
   And sleep and snore, and rend apparel out; —
   Why, Jessica, I say!
LAUNCELOT GOBBO.
                              Why, Jessica!
SHYLOCK.
   Who bids thee call? I do not bid thee call.
LAUNCELOT GOBBO.
   Your worship was wont to tell me that I could
   do nothing without bidding.

Enter JESSICA.

JESSICA.
   Call you? what is your will?
SHYLOCK.
   I am bid forth to supper, Jessica:
   There are my keys. — But wherefore should I
   go?

51

I am not bid for love; they flatter me:
But yet I'll go in hate, to feed upon
The prodigal Christian. — Jessica, my girl,
Look to my house. — I am right loth to go:
There is some ill a-brewing towards my rest,
For I did dream of money-bags tonight.

LAUNCELOT GOBBO.

I beseech you, sir, go: my young master doth
expect your reproach.

SHYLOCK.

So do I his.

LAUNCELOT GOBBO.

And they have conspired together, — I will
not say you shall see a mask; but if you
do, then it was not for nothing that my
nose fell a-bleeding on Black-Monday last at
six o'clock i' th' morning, falling out that
year on Ash-Wednesday was four year, in th'
afternoon.

SHYLOCK.

What, are there masks? — Hear you me, Jessica:
Lock up my doors; and when you hear the
drum,
And the vile squealing of the wry-neck'd fife,
Clamber not you up to the casements then,
Nor thrust your head into the public street,
To gaze on Christian fools with varnish'd
faces;
But stop my house's ears, I mean my casements:
Let not the sound of shallow foppery enter
My sober house. — By Jacob's staff, I swear
I have no mind of feasting forth tonight:

But I will go. — Go you before me, sirrah;
Say I will come.
LAUNCELOT GOBBO.

    I will go before, sir. —
Mistress, look out at window for all this;
  There will come a Christian by
  Will be worth a Jewess' eye.

          [*Exit.*

SHYLOCK.
What says that fool of Hagar's offspring, ha?
JESSICA.
His words were, 'Farewell, mistress;' nothing
else.
SHYLOCK.
The patch is kind enough; but a huge feeder,
Snail-slow in profit, and he sleeps by day
More than the wild-cat: drones hive not with
me;
Therefore I part with him; and part with him
To one that I would have him help to waste
His borrow'd purse. — Well, Jessica, go in:
Perhaps I will return immediately:
Do as I bid you; shut doors after you:
Fast bind, fast find, —
A proverb never stale in thrifty mind.

          [*Exit.*

JESSICA.
Farewell; and if my fortune be not cross'd,
I have a father, you a daughter, lost.

          [*Exit.*

Enter the Maskers GRATIANO *and* SALARINO.

GRATIANO.

This is the pent-house under which Lorenzo
Desired us to make stand.

SALARINO.

His hour is almost past.

GRATIANO.

And it is marvel he out-dwells his hour,
For lovers ever run before the clock.

SALARINO.

O, ten times faster Venus' pigeons fly
To seal love's bonds new-made than they are
wont
To keep obliged faith unforfeited!

GRATIANO.

That ever holds: who riseth from a feast
With that keen appetite that he sits down?
Where is the horse that doth untread again
His tedious measures with the unbated fire
That he did pace them first? All things that
are,
Are with more spirit chased than enjoy'd.
How like a younker or a prodigal
The scarfed bark puts from her native bay,
Hugg'd and embraced by the strumpet wind!
How like a prodigal doth she return,
With over-weather'd ribs, and ragged sails,
Lean, rent, and beggar'd by the strumpet
wind!

SALARINO.

Here comes Lorenzo: — more of this hereafter.

Enter LORENZO.

54

LORENZO.

Sweet friends, your patience for my long abode;
Not I, but my affairs, have made you wait:
When you shall please to play the thieves for
wives,
I'll watch as long for you then. — Approach;
Here dwells my father Jew. — Ho! who's within?

Enter JESSICA, *above, in boy's clothes.*

JESSICA.

Who are you? Tell me, for more certainty,
Albeit I'll swear that I do know your tongue.

LORENZO.

Lorenzo, and thy love.

JESSICA.

Lorenzo, certain; and my love, indeed, —
For who love I so much? And now who knows
But you, Lorenzo, whether I am yours?

LORENZO.

Heaven and thy thoughts are witness that thou
art.

JESSICA.

Here, catch this casket; it is worth the pains.
I am glad 'tis night, you do not look on me,
For I am much ashamed of my exchange:
But love is blind, and lovers cannot see
The pretty follies that themselves commit;
For if they could, Cupid himself would blush
To see me thus transformed to a boy.

LORENZO.

Descend, for you must be my torch-bearer.

JESSICA.

What, must I hold a candle to my shames?
They in themselves, good sooth, are too-too
light.
Why, 'tis an office of discovery, love;
And I should be obscured.

LORENZO.

So are you, sweet,
Even in the lovely garnish of a boy.
But come at once;
For the close night doth play the runaway,
And we are stay'd for at Bassanio's feast.

JESSICA.

I will make fast the doors, and gild myself
With some moe ducats, and be with you
straight.

[Exit above.

GRATIANO.

Now, by my hood, a Gentile, and no Jew.

LORENZO.

Beshrew me but I love her heartily;
For she is wise, if I can judge of her;
And fair she is, if that mine eyes be true;
And true she is, as she hath proved herself;
And therefore, like herself, wise, fair, and true,
Shall she be placed in my constant soul.

Enter JESSICA, *below.*

What, art thou come? — On, gentlemen; away!
Our masking mates by this time for us stay.

[Exit with JESSICA *and* SALARINO.

56

Enter ANTONIO.

ANTONIO.
  Who's there?
GRATIANO.
  Signior Antonio!
ANTONIO.
  Fie, fie, Gratiano! where are all the rest?
  'Tis nine o'clock; our friends all stay for you.
  No mask tonight: the wind is come about;
  Bassanio presently will go aboard:
  I have sent twenty out to seek for you.
GRATIANO.
  I am glad on't: I desire no more delight
  Than to be under sail and gone tonight.
                                    [*Exeunt.*

Scene VI.

Belmont. A room in PORTIA'S house.
Enter PORTIA, *with the* PRINCE OF MOROCCO,
and their TRAINS. *Flourish cornets.*

PORTIA.
  Go draw aside the curtains, and discover
  The several caskets to this noble prince. —
  Now make your choice.
PRINCE OF MOROCCO.
  The first, of gold, which this inscription
  bears, —
  'Who chooseth me shall gain what many men
  desire;'
  The second, silver, which this promise carries, —
  'Who chooseth me shall get as much as he
  deserves;'
  This third, dull lead, with warning all as
  blunt, —
  'Who chooseth me must give and hazard all
  he hath.' —
  How shall I know if I do choose the right?
PORTIA.
  The one of them contains my picture, prince:
  If you choose that, then I am yours withal.
PRINCE OF MOROCCO.
  Some god direct my judgement! Let me see;

I will survey the inscriptions back again.
What says this leaden casket?
'Who chooseth me must give and hazard all
he hath.'
Must give, — for what? for lead? hazard for
lead?
This casket threatens: men that hazard all
Do it in hope of fair advantages:
A golden mind stoops not to shows of dross;
I'll then nor give nor hazard aught for lead.
What says the silver, with her virgin hue?
'Who chooseth me shall get as much as he
deserves.'
As much as he deserves! — Pause there, Morocco,
And weigh thy value with an even hand:
If thou be'st rated by thy estimation,
Thou dost deserve enough; and yet enough
May not extend so far as to the lady:
And yet to be afeard of my deserving,
Were but a weak disabling of myself.
As much as I deserve! — Why, that's the lady:
I do in birth deserve her, and in fortunes,
In graces, and in qualities of breeding;
But more than these, in love I do deserve.
What if I stray'd no further, but chose here? —
Let's see once more this saying graved in
gold:
'Who chooseth me shall gain what many men
desire.'
Why, that's the lady; all the world desires her;
From the four corners of the earth they come,
To kiss this shrine, this mortal-breathing saint:

The Hyrcanian deserts and the vasty wilds
Of wide Arabia are as throughfares now
For princes to come view fair Portia:
The watery kingdom, whose ambitious head
Spits in the face of heaven, is no bar
To stop the foreign spirits; but they come,
As o'er a brook, to see fair Portia.
One of these three contains her heavenly
picture.
Is't like that lead contains her? 'Twere damnation
To think so base a thought: it were too gross
To rib her cerecloth in the obscure grave.
Or shall I think in silver she's immured,
Being ten times undervalued to tried gold?
O sinful thought! Never so rich a gem
Was set in worse than gold. They have in
England
A coin that bears the figure of an angel
Stamped in gold, — but that's insculpt upon;
But here an angel in a golden bed
Lies all within. — Deliver me the key:
Here do I choose, and thrive I as I may!

PORTIA.
There, take it, prince; and if my form lie
there,
Then I am yours.
                          [*He opens the golden casket.*

PRINCE OF MOROCCO.
                          O hell! what have we here?
A carrion Death, within whose empty eye
There is a written scroll! I'll read the writing.

All that glisters is not gold, —
Often have you heard that told:
Many a man his life hath sold
But my outside to behold:
Gilded tombs do worms infold.
Had you been as wise as bold,
Young in limbs, in judgement old,
Your answer had not been inscroll'd:
Fare you well; your suit is cold.

Cold, indeed; and labour lost:
Then, farewell, heat; and welcome, frost! —
Portia, adieu. I have too grieved a heart
To take a tedious leave: thus losers part.

        [*Exit with his* TRAIN. *Cornets.*

PORTIA.

A gentle riddance. — Draw the curtains, go. —
Let all of his complexion choose me so.

        [*Exeunt.*

Scene VII.

Venice. A street.
Enter SALARINO *and* SOLANIO.

SALARINO.
Why, man, I saw Bassanio under sail:
With him is Gratiano gone along;
And in their ship I am sure Lorenzo is not.
SOLANIO.
The villain Jew with outcries raised the duke;
Who went with him to search Bassanio's ship.
SALARINO.
He came too late, the ship was under sail:
But there the duke was given to understand
That in a gondola were seen together
Lorenzo and his amorous Jessica:
Besides, Antonio certified the duke
They were not with Bassanio in his ship.
SOLANIO.
I never heard a passion so confused,
So strange, outrageous, and so variable,
As the dog Jew did utter in the streets:
'My daughter! – O my ducats! – O my
daughter!
Fled with a Christian! – O my Christian
ducats! –
Justice! the law! my ducats, and my daughter!

63

A sealed bag, two sealed bags of ducats,
Of double ducats, stol'n from me by my
daughter!
And jewels, — two stones, two rich and precious
stones,
Stol'n by my daughter! — Justice! find the
girl!
She hath the stones upon her, and the ducats!'

SALARINO.

Why, all the boys in Venice follow him,
Crying, — his stones, his daughter, and his
ducats.

SOLANIO.

Let good Antonio look he keep his day,
Or he shall pay for this.

SALARINO.

             Marry, well remember'd,
I reason'd with a Frenchman yesterday,
Who told me, — in the narrow seas that part
The French and English, there miscarried
A vessel of our country richly fraught:
I thought upon Antonio when he told me;
And wish'd in silence that it were not his.

SOLANIO.

You were best to tell Antonio what you hear;
Yet do not suddenly, for it may grieve him.

SALARINO.

A kinder gentleman treads not the earth.
I saw Bassanio and Antonio part:
Bassanio told him he would make some speed
Of his return: he answer'd, 'Do not so, —
Slubber not business for my sake, Bassanio,

But stay the very riping of the time;
And for the Jew's bond which he hath of me,
Let it not enter in your mind of love:
Be merry; and employ your chiefest thoughts
To courtship, and such fair ostents of love
As shall conveniently become you there:'
And even there, his eye being big with tears,
Turning his face, he put his hand behind him,
And with affection wondrous sensible
He wrung Bassanio's hand; and so they parted.

SOLANIO.
I think he only loves the world for him.
I pray thee, let us go and find him out,
And quicken his embraced heaviness
With some delight or other.

SALARINO.
                       Do we so.
                             [*Exeunt.*

Scene VIII.

Belmont. A room in PORTIA'S house.
Enter NERISSA *and a* SERVITOR.

NERISSA.
Quick, quick, I pray thee; draw the curtain
straight:
The Prince of Arragon hath ta'en his oath,
And comes to his election presently.

Enter PRINCE OF ARRAGON, *his* TRAIN, *and*
PORTIA. *Flourish cornets.*

PORTIA.
Behold, there stand the caskets, noble prince:
If you choose that wherein I am contain'd,
Straight shall our nuptial rites be solemnized:
But if you fail, without more speech, my lord,
You must be gone from hence immediately.
PRINCE OF ARRAGON.
I am enjoin'd by oath to observe three things: —
First, never to unfold to any one
Which casket 'twas I chose; next, if I fail
Of the right casket, never in my life
To woo a maid in way of marriage; lastly,
If I do fail in fortune of my choice,
Immediately to leave you and be gone.

67

PORTIA.

    To these injunctions every one doth swear
    That comes to hazard for my worthless self.

PRINCE OF ARRAGON.

    And so have I address'd me. Fortune now
    To my heart's hope! — Gold, silver, and base
    lead.
    'Who chooseth me must give and hazard all
    he hath.'
    You shall look fairer, ere I give or hazard.
    What says the golden chest? ha! let me see:
    'Who chooseth me shall gain what many men
    desire.'
    What many men desire! — that many may be
    meant
    By the fool multitude, that choose by show,
    Not learning more than the fond eye doth
    teach;
    Which pries not to th' interior, but, like the
    martlet,
    Builds in the weather on the outward wall,
    Even in the force and road of casualty.
    I will not choose what many men desire,
    Because I will not jump with common spirits,
    And rank me with the barbarous multitudes.
    Why, then to thee, thou silver treasure-house;
    Tell me once more what title thou dost bear:
    'Who chooseth me shall get as much as he
    deserves:'
    And well said too; for who shall go about
    To cozen fortune, and be honourable
    Without the stamp of merit? Let none presume

To wear an undeserved dignity.
O, that estates, degrees, and offices,
Were not derived corruptly! and that clear
honour
Were purchased by the merit of the wearer!
How many then should cover that stand bare!
How many be commanded that command!
How much low peasantry would then be
glean'd
From the true seed of honour! and how much
honour
Pick'd from the chaff and ruin of the times,
To be new-varnish'd! Well, but to my choice:
'Who chooseth me shall get as much as he
deserves.'
I will assume desert. − Give me a key for
this,
And instantly unlock my fortunes here.
                    [*He opens the silver casket.*
PORTIA [*aside*].
Too long a pause for that which you find here.
PRINCE OF ARRAGON.
What's here? the portrait of a blinking idiot,
Presenting me a schedule! I will read it.
How much unlike art thou to Portia!
How much unlike my hopes and my deservings!
'Who chooseth me shall have as much as he
deserves.'
Did I deserve no more than a fool's head?
Is that my prize? are my deserts no better?
PORTIA.
To offend, and judge, are distinct offices,

And of opposed natures.

PRINCE OF ARRAGON.

What is here?

The fire seven times tried this:
Seven times tried that judgement is,
That did never choose amiss.
Some there be that shadows kiss.
Such have but a shadow's bliss.
There be fools alive, I wis,
Silver'd o'er; and so was this.
Take what wife you will to bed,
I will ever be your head:
So be gone; you are sped.

Still more fool I shall appear
By the time I linger here:
With one fool's head I came to woo,
But I go away with two. —
Sweet, adieu. I'll keep my oath,
Patiently to bear my wroth.

[*Exit with his* TRAIN.

PORTIA.

Thus hath the candle singed the moth.
O, these deliberate fools! when they do choose,
They have the wisdom by their wit to lose.

NERISSA.

The ancient saying is no heresy, —
Hanging and wiving goes by destiny.

PORTIA.

Come, draw the curtain, Nerissa.

Enter a SERVANT.

SERVANT.
  Where is my lady?
PORTIA.
                    Here: what would my lord?

SERVANT.
  Madam, there is alighted at your gate
  A young Venetian, one that comes before
  To signify th' approaching of his lord;
  From whom he bringeth sensible regreets,
  To wit, besides commends and courteous breath,
  Gifts of rich value. Yet I have not seen
  So likely an ambassador of love:
  A day in April never came so sweet,
  To show how costly summer was at hand,
  As this fore-spurrer comes before his lord.
PORTIA.
  No more, I pray thee: I am half afeard
  Thou wilt say anon he is some kin to thee,
  Thou spend'st such high-day wit in praising
  him. —
  Come, come, Nerissa; for I long to see
  Quick Cupid's post that comes so mannerly.
NERISSA.
  Bassanio, lord Love, if thy will it be!
                              [*Exeunt.*

ACT III

Scene I.

Venice. A street.
Enter SOLANIO *and* SALARINO.

SOLANIO.
Now, what news on the Rialto?
SOLANIO.
Why, yet it lives there uncheck'd, that Antonio hath a ship of rich lading wrack'd on the narrow seas; the Goodwins, I think they call the place; a very dangerous flat and fatal, where the carcasses of many a tall ship lie buried, as they say, if my gossip Report be an honest woman of her word.
SOLANIO.
I would she were as lying a gossip in that as ever knapt ginger, or made her neighbours believe she wept for the death of a third husband. But it is true, – without any slips of prolixity, or crossing the plain highway of talk, – that the good Antonio, the honest Antonio, – O, that I had a title good enough to keep his name company! –
SALARINO.
Come, the full stop.
SOLANIO.
Ha, – what sayest thou? – Why, the end is,

he hath lost a ship.

SALARINO.

I would it might prove the end of his losses.

SOLANIO.

Let me say amen betimes, lest the devil cross
my prayer, — for here he comes in the likeness
of a Jew.

Enter SHYLOCK.

How now, Shylock! what news among the
merchants?

SHYLOCK.

You knew, none so well, none so well as you,
of my daughter's flight.

SALARINO.

That's certain: I, for my part, knew the tailor
that made the wings she flew withal.

SOLANIO.

And Shylock, for his own part, knew the bird
was fledged; and then it is the complexion of
them all to leave the dam.

SHYLOCK.

She is damn'd for it.

SALARINO.

That's certain, if the devil may be her judge.

SHYLOCK.

My own flesh and blood to rebel!

SOLANIO.

Out upon it, old carrion! rebels it at these
years?

SHYLOCK.

I say my daughter is my flesh and blood.

SALARINO.

There is more difference between thy flesh and hers than between jet and ivory; more between your bloods than there is between red wine and rhenish. — But tell us, do you hear whether Antonio have had any loss at sea or no?

SHYLOCK.

There I have another bad match: a bankrupt, a prodigal, who dare scarce show his head on the Rialto; — a beggar, that was used to come so smug upon the mart; — let him look to his bond: he was wont to lend money for a Christian courtesy: — let him look to his bond.

SALARINO.

Why, I am sure, if he forfeit, thou wilt not take his flesh: what's that good for?

SHYLOCK.

To bait fish withal: if it will feed nothing else, it will feed my revenge. He hath disgraced me, and hinder'd me half a million; laugh'd at my losses, mock'd at my gains, scorn'd my nation, thwarted my bargains, cooled my friends, heated mine enemies: and what's his reason? I am a Jew. Hath not a Jew eyes? hath not a Jew hands, organs, dimensions, senses, affections, passions? fed with the same food, hurt with the same weapons, subject to the same diseases, heal'd by the same means, warm'd and cool'd by the same winter and summer, as a Christian is? If you prick us, do we not bleed? if you tickle us, do we not laugh? if you poison us, do we not die? and if you wrong us, shall we not revenge? if we are like you in the rest, we will resemble you in that. If a Jew wrong a Christian, what is his humility? revenge: if a Christian wrong a Jew, what should his sufferance be by Christian example? why, revenge. The villainy you teach me, I will execute; and it shall go hard but I will better the instruction.

Enter a SERVANT *from* ANTONIO.

SERVANT.
Gentlemen, my master Antonio is at his house, and desires to speak with you both.
SALARINO.
We have been up and down to seek him.
SOLANIO.
Here comes another of the tribe: a third cannot be match'd, unless the devil himself turn Jew.
    [*Exeunt* SOLANIO, SALARINO *and* SERVANT.

Enter TUBAL.

SHYLOCK.
How now, Tubal! What news from Genoa? hast thou found my daughter?
TUBAL.
I often came where I did hear of her, but cannot find her.

SHYLOCK.

Why, there, there, there, there! a diamond gone, cost me two thousand ducats in Frankfort! The curse never fell upon our nation till now; I never felt it till now: — two thousand ducats in that; and other precious, precious jewels. — I would my daughter were dead at my foot, and the jewels in her ear! would she were hearsed at my foot, and the ducats in her coffin! No news of them? — Why, so: — and I know not what's spent in the search: why, thou, loss upon loss! the thief gone with so much, and so much to find the thief; and no satisfaction, no revenge: nor no ill luck stirring but what lights on my shoulders; no sighs but of my breathing; no tears but of my shedding.

TUBAL.

Yes, other men have ill luck too: Antonio, as I heard in Genoa, —

SHYLOCK.

What, what, what? ill luck, ill luck?

TUBAL.

Hath an argosy cast away, coming from Tripolis.

SHYLOCK.

I thank God, I thank God! — Is't true, is't true?

TUBAL.

I spoke with some of the sailors that escaped the wrack.

SHYLOCK

I thank thee, good Tubal: — good news, good news! ha, ha! — where? in Genoa?

TUBAL.

Your daughter spent in Genoa, as I heard, one night fourscore ducats.

SHYLOCK.

Thou stick'st a dagger in me: — I shall never see my gold again: fourscore ducats at a sitting! fourscore ducats!

TUBAL.

There came divers of Antonio's creditors in my company to Venice, that swear he cannot choose but break.

SHYLOCK.

I am very glad of it: — I'll plague him; I'll torture him: — I am glad on't.

TUBAL.

One of them show'd me a ring that he had of your daughter for a monkey.

SHYLOCK.

Out upon her! Thou torturest me, Tubal: it was my turquoise; I had it of Leah when I was a bachelor: I would not have given it for a wilderness of monkeys.

TUBAL.

But Antonio is certainly undone.

SHYLOCK.

Nay, that's true, that's very true. Go, Tubal, fee me an officer; bespeak him a fortnight before. I will have the heart of him, if he forfeit; for, were he out of Venice, I can make what merchandise I will. Go, Tubal, and meet me at our synagogue; go, good Tubal; at our synagogue, Tubal.

[Exeunt.

Scene II.

Belmont. A room in PORTIA'S house.

Enter BASSANIO, PORTIA, GRATIANO, NERISSA, *and all their* TRAIN.

PORTIA.
    I pray you, tarry: pause a day or two
    Before you hazard; for, in choosing wrong,
    I lose your company: therefore, forbear awhile.
    There's something tells me — but it is not love —
    I would not lose you; and you know yourself,
    Hate counsels not in such a quality.
    But lest you should not understand me well, —
    And yet a maiden hath no tongue but thought, —
    I would detain you here some month or two
    Before you venture for me. I could teach you
    How to choose right, but then I am forsworn;
    So will I never be: so may you miss me;
    But if you do, you'll make me wish a sin,
    That I had been forsworn. Beshrew your eyes,
    They have o'erlook'd me, and divided me;
    One half of me is yours, the other half yours, —
    Mine own, I would say; but if mine, then yours,

And so all yours! O, these naughty times
Put bars between the owners and their rights!
And so, though yours, not yours. — Prove it
so,
Let fortune go to hell for it, — not I.
I speak too long; but 'tis to peize the time,
To eke it, and to draw it out in length,
To stay you from election.
BASSANIO.

                                Let me choose;
For, as I am, I live upon the rack.
PORTIA.
Upon the rack, Bassanio! then confess
What treason there is mingled with your love.
BASSANIO.
None but that ugly treason of mistrust,
Which makes me fear the enjoying of my love:
There may as well be amity and league
'Tween snow and fire, as treason and my love.
PORTIA.
Ay, but I fear you speak upon the rack,
Where men enforced do speak any thing.
BASSANIO.
Promise me life, and I'll confess the truth.
PORTIA.
Well then, confess, and live.
BASSANIO.

                        'Confess,' and 'love,'
Had been the very sum of my confession:
O happy torment, when my torturer
Doth teach me answers for deliverance!
But let me to my fortune and the caskets.

PORTIA.
    Away, then! I am lock'd in one of them:
    If you do love me, you will find me out. —
    Nerissa, and the rest, stand all aloof. —
    Let music sound while he doth make his
    choice;
    Then, if he lose, he makes a swan-like end,
    Fading in music: that the comparison
    May stand more proper, my eye shall be the
    stream
    And watery death-bed for him. He may win;
    And what is music then? then music is
    Even as the flourish when true subjects bow
    To a new-crowned monarch: such it is
    As are those dulcet sounds in break of day
    That creep into the dreaming bridegroom's
    ear,
    And summon him to marriage. — Now he
    goes,
    With no less presence, but with much more
    love,
    Than young Alcides, when he did redeem
    The virgin tribute paid by howling Troy
    To the sea-monster: I stand for sacrifice;
    The rest aloof are the Dardanian wives,
    With bleared visages, come forth to view
    The issue of th' exploit. Go, Hercules!
    Live thou, I live: — with much much more
    dismay
    I view the fight than thou that makest the fray.
Here Music. — A Song, the whilst BASSANIO
    comments on the caskets to himself.

Tell me where is fancy bred,
Or in the heart or in the head?
How begot, how nourished?
   Reply, reply.
It is engender'd in the eyes,
With gazing fed; and fancy dies
In the cradle where it lies.
   Let us all ring fancy's knell;
   I'll begin it, — Ding, dong, bell.

   All. Ding, dong, bell.

BASSANIO.
So may the outward shows be least themselves:
The world is still deceived with ornament.
In law, what plea so tainted and corrupt,
But, being season'd with a gracious voice,
Obscures the show of evil? In religion,
What damned error, but some sober brow
Will bless it, and approve it with a text,
Hiding the grossness with fair ornament?
There is no vice so simple, but assumes
Some mark of virtue on his outward parts:
How many cowards, whose hearts are all as false
As stairs of sand, wear yet upon their chins
The beards of Hercules and frowning Mars;
Who, inward search'd, have livers white as milk;
And these assume but valour's excrement
To render them redoubted! Look on beauty,
And you shall see 'tis purchased by the weight;
Which therein works a miracle in nature,

Making them lightest that wear most of it:
So are those crisped snaky golden locks,
Which make such wanton gambols with the
wind,
Upon supposed fairness, often known
To be the dowry of a second head,
The skull that bred them in the sepulchre.
Thus ornament is but the guiled shore
To a most dangerous sea; the beauteous scarf
Veiling an Indian beauty; in a word,
The seeming truth which cunning times put
on
To entrap the wisest. Therefore, thou gaudy
gold,
Hard food for Midas, I will none of thee;
Nor none of thee, thou stale and common
drudge
'Tween man and man: but thou, thou meagre
lead,
Which rather threatenest than dost promise
aught,
Thy paleness moves me more than eloquence;
And here choose I: — joy be the consequence!
PORTIA [aside].
How all the other passions fleet to air, —
As doubtful thoughts, and rash-embraced despair,
And shuddering fear, and green-eyed jealousy!
O love, be moderate; allay thy ecstasy;
In measure rain thy joy; scant this excess!
I feel too much thy blessing: make it less,
For fear I surfeit!

BASSANIO.

What find I here?

[*Opening the leaden casket.*

Fair Portia's counterfeit! What demi-god
Hath come so near creation? Move these eyes?
Or whether, riding on the balls of mine,
Seem they in motion? Here are sever'd lips,
Parted with sugar breath: so sweet a bar
Should sunder such sweet friends. Here in her
hairs
The painter plays the spider; and hath woven
A golden mesh t'entrap the hearts of men,
Faster than gnats in cobwebs: but her eyes, —
How could he see to do them? having made
one,
Methinks it should have power to steal both
his,
And leave itself unfurnish'd. Yet look, how far
The substance of my praise doth wrong this
shadow
In underprizing it, so far this shadow
Doth limp behind the substance. — Here's the
scroll,
The continent and summary of my fortune.

You that choose not by the view,
Chance as fair, and choose as true!
Since this fortune falls to you,
Be content, and seek no new.
If you be well pleased with this,
And hold your fortune for your bliss,
Turn you where your lady is,

And claim her with a loving kiss.

A gentle scroll. — Fair lady, by your leave;
                                    [*Kissing her.*
I come by note, to give and to receive.
Like one of two contending in a prize,
That thinks he hath done well in people's eyes,
Hearing applause and universal shout,
Giddy in spirit, still gazing in a doubt
Whether those peals of praise be his or no;
So, thrice-fair lady, stand I, even so;
As doubtful whether what I see be true,
Until confirm'd, sign'd, ratified by you.

PORTIA.
You see me, Lord Bassanio, where I stand,
Such as I am: though for myself alone
I would not be ambitious in my wish,
To wish myself much better; yet for you
I would be trebled twenty times myself;
A thousand times more fair, ten thousand times
more rich;
That, only to stand high in your account,
I might in virtues, beauties, livings, friends,
Exceed account: but the full sum of me
Is sum of nothing; which, to term in gross,
Is an unlesson'd girl, unschool'd, unpractised:
Happy in this, she is not yet so old
But she may learn; happier than this,
She is not bred so dull but she can learn;
Happiest of all is that her gentle spirit
Commits itself to yours to be directed,
As from her lord, her governor, her king.

Myself and what is mine to you and yours
Is now converted: but now I was the lord
Of this fair mansion, master of my servants,
Queen o'er myself; and even now, but now,
This house, these servants, and this same
myself,
Are yours, my lord: I give them with this ring;
Which when you part from, lose, or give away,
Let it presage the ruin of your love,
And be my vantage to exclaim on you.

BASSANIO.

Madam, you have bereft me of all words,
Only my blood speaks to you in my veins:
And there is such confusion in my powers,
As, after some oration fairly spoke
By a beloved prince, there doth appear
Among the buzzing pleased multitude;
Where every something, being blent together,
Turns to a wild of nothing, save of joy,
Express'd and not express'd. But when the ring
Parts from this finger, then parts life from
hence:
O, then be bold to say Bassanio's dead!

NERISSA.

My lord and lady, it is now our time,
That have stood by, and seen our wishes
prosper,
To cry, good joy: — good joy, my lord and
lady!

GRATIANO.

My Lord Bassanio and my gentle lady,
I wish you all the joy that you can wish;

For I am sure you can wish none from me:
And, when your honours mean to solemnize
The bargain of your faith, I do beseech you,
Even at that time I may be married too.

BASSANIO.

With all my heart, so thou canst get a wife.

GRATIANO.

I thank your lordship, you have got me one.
My eyes, my lord, can look as swift as yours:
You saw the mistress, I beheld the maid;
You loved, I loved; for intermission
No more pertains to me, my lord, than you.
Your fortune stood upon the caskets there;
And so did mine too, as the matter falls;
For wooing here, until I sweat again,
And swearing, till my very roof was dry
With oaths of love, at last, — if promise last, —
I got a promise of this fair one here,
To have her love, provided that your fortune
Achieved her mistress.

PORTIA.

                        Is this true, Nerissa?

NERISSA.

Madam, it is, so you stand pleased withal.

BASSANIO.

And do you, Gratiano, mean good faith?

GRATIANO.

Yes, faith, my lord.

BASSANIO.

Our feast shall be much honour'd in your marriage.

GRATIANO.

We'll play with them the first boy for a
thousand ducats.

NERISSA.

What, and stake down?

GRATIANO.

No; we shall ne'er win at that sport, and stake
down. —
But who comes here? Lorenzo and his infidel?
What, and my old Venetian friend Solanio?

Enter LORENZO, JESSICA, *and* SOLANIO.

BASSANIO.

Lorenzo and Solanio, welcome hither;
If that the youth of my new interest here
Have power to bid you welcome. — By your
leave,
I bid my very friends and countrymen,
Sweet Portia, welcome.

PORTIA.

               So do I, my lord;
They are entirely welcome.

LORENZO.

I thank your honour. — For my part, my lord,
My purpose was not to have seen you here;
But meeting with Solanio by the way,
He did entreat me, past all saying nay,
To come with him along.

SOLANIO.

               I did, my lord;
And I have reason for't. Signior Antonio

Commends him to you.

[Gives BASSANIO *a letter.*

BASSANIO.

Ere I ope his letter,
I pray you, tell me how my good friend doth.

SOLANIO.

Not sick, my lord, unless it be in mind;
Not well, unless in mind: his letter there
Will show you his estate.

*[*BASSANIO *reads the letter.*

GRATIANO.

Nerissa, cheer you stranger; bid her welcome. —
Your hand, Solanio: what's the news from
Venice?
How doth that royal merchant, good Antonio?
I know he will be glad of our success;
We are the Jasons, we have won the fleece.

SOLANIO.

I would you had won the fleece that he hath
lost!

PORTIA.

There are some shrewd contents in yon same
paper,
That steals the colour from Bassanio's cheek:
Some dear friend dead; else nothing in the
world
Could turn so much the constitution
Of any constant man. What, worse and worse! —
With leave, Bassanio; I am half yourself,
And I must freely have the half of any thing
That this same paper brings you.

BASSANIO.

O sweet Portia,
Here are a few of the unpleasnt'st words
That ever blotted paper! Gentle lady,
When I did first impart my love to you,
I freely told you, all the wealth I had
Ran in my veins, — I was a gentleman;
And then I told you true: and yet, dear lady,
Rating myself at nothing, you shall see
How much I was a braggart. When I told you
My state was nothing, I should then have told
you
That I was worse than nothing, for, indeed,
I have engaged myself to a dear friend,
Engaged my friend to his mere enemy,
To feed my means. Here is a letter, lady, —
The paper as the body of my friend,
And every word in it a gaping wound,
Issuing life-blood. — But is it true, Solanio?
Have all his ventures fail'd? What, not one
hit?
From Tripolis, from Mexico, and England,
From Lisbon, Barbary, and India?
And not one vessel scape the dreadful touch
Of merchant-marring rocks?

SOLANIO.

Not one, my lord.
Besides, it should appear, that if he had
The present money to discharge the Jew,
He would not take it. Never did I know
A creature, that did bear the shape of man,
So keen and greedy to confound a man;

He plies the duke at morning and at night;
And doth impeach the freedom of the state,
If they deny him justice: twenty merchants,
The duke himself, and the magnificoes
Of greatest port, have all persuaded with him;
But none can drive him from the envious plea
Of forfeiture, of justice, and his bond.

JESSICA.

When I was with him, I have heard him swear,
To Tubal and to Chus, his countrymen,
That he would rather have Antonio's flesh
That twenty times the value of the sum
That he did owe him: and I know, my lord,
If law, authority, and power deny not,
It will go hard with poor Antonio.

PORTIA.

Is it your dear friend that is thus in trouble?

BASSANIO.

The dearest friend to me, the kindest man,
The best-condition'd and unwearied spirit
In doing courtesies; and one in whom
The ancient Roman honour more appears
Than any that draws breath in Italy.

PORTIA.

What sum owes he the Jew?

BASSANIO.

For me three thousand ducats.

PORTIA.

                                    What, no more?
Pay him six thousand, and deface the bond;
Double six thousand, and then treble that,
Before a friend of this description

Shall lose a hair through Bassanio's fault.
First go with me to church and call me wife,
And then away to Venice to your friend;
For never shall you lie by Portia's side
With an unquiet soul. You shall have gold
To pay the petty debt twenty times over:
When it is paid, bring your true friend along.
My maid Nerissa and myself meantime
Will live as maids and widows. Come away!
For you shall hence upon your wedding-day:
Bid your friends welcome, show a merry cheer:
Since you are dear-bought, I will love you
dear. —
But let me hear the letter of your friend.

BASSANIO [*reads*].

Sweet Bassanio, my ships have all miscarried, my
creditors grow cruel, my estate is very low, my
bond to the Jew is forfeit; and since in paying
it, it is impossible I should live, all debts are
clear'd between you and I, if I might but see
you at my death. Notwithstanding, use your
pleasure: if your love do not persuade you to
come, let not my letter.

PORTIA.

O love, dispatch all business, and be gone!

BASSANIO.

Since I have your good leave to go away,
    I will make haste: but, till I come again,
No bed shall e'er be guilty of my stay,
    No rest be interposer 'twixt us twain.

                                        [*Exeunt.*

Scene III.

Enter SHYLOCK, SALARINO, ANTONIO, *and*
GAOLER.

SHYLOCK.
  Gaoler, look to him: — tell not me of mercy; —
  This is the fool that lent out money gratis: —
  Gaoler, look to him.
ANTONIO.
                    Hear me yet, good Shylock.
SHYLOCK.
  I'll have my bond; speak not against my bond:
  I have sworn an oath that I will have my bond.
  Thou call'dst me dog before thou hadst a
  cause;
  But, since I am a dog, beware my fangs:
  The duke shall grant me justice. — I do wonder,
  Thou naughty gaoler, that thou art so fond
  To come abroad with him at his request.
ANTONIO.
  I pray thee, hear me speak.
SHYLOCK.
  I'll have my bond; I will not hear thee speak:
  I'll have my bond; and therefore speak no
  more.
  I'll not be made a soft and dull-eyed fool,

95

To shake the head, relent, and sigh, and yield
To Christian intercessors. Follow not;
I'll have no speaking: I will have my bond.

                                                    [*Exit.*

SALARINO.
  It is the most impenetrable cur
  That ever kept with men.
ANTONIO.
                                        Let him alone:
  I'll follow him no more with bootless prayers.
  He seeks my life; his reason well I know:
  I oft deliver'd from his forfeitures
  Many that have at times made moan to me;
  Therefore he hates me.
SALARINO.
                                        I am sure the duke
  Will never grant this forfeiture to hold.
ANTONIO.
  The duke cannot deny the course of law;
  For the commodity that strangers have
  With us in Venice, if it be denied,
  Will much impeach the justice of the state;
  Since that the trade and profit of the city
  Consisteth of all nations. Therefore, go:
  These griefs and losses have so bated me,
  That I shall hardly spare a pound of flesh
  To-morrow to my bloody creditor. —
  Well, gaoler, on. — Pray God, Bassanio come
  To see me pay his debt, — and then I care
  not!

                                                    [*Exeunt.*

Scene IV.

Belmont. A room in PORTIA'S house.
Enter PORTIA, NERISSA, LORENZO, JESSICA,
and BALTHAZAR, *a man of* PORTIA'S.

LORENZO.

Madam, although I speak it in your presence,
You have a noble and a true conceit
Of god-like amity; which appears most strongly
In bearing thus the absence of your lord.
But if you knew to whom you show this
honour,
How true a gentleman you send relief,
How dear a lover of my lord your husband,
I know you would be prouder of the work
Than customary bounty can enforce you.

PORTIA.

I never did repent for doing good,
Nor shall not now: for in companions
That do converse and waste the time together,
Whose souls do bear an equal yoke of love,
There must be needs a like proportion
Of lineaments, of manners, and of spirit;
Which makes me think that this Antonio,
Being the bosom lover of my lord,
Must needs be like my lord. If it be so,
How little is the cost I have bestow'd

In purchasing the semblance of my soul
From out the state of hellish cruelty!
This comes too near the praising of myself;
Therefore no more of it: hear other things. —
Lorenzo, I commit into your hands
The husbandry and manage of my house
Until my lord's return: for mine own part,
I have toward heaven breathed a secret vow
To live in prayer and contemplation,
Only attended by Nerissa here,
Until her husband and my lord's return:
There is a monastery two miles off;
And there will we abide. I do desire you
Not to deny this imposition;
The which my love and some necessity
Now lays upon you.

LORENZO.

                        Madam, with all my heart;
I shall obey you in all fair commands.

PORTIA.

My people do already know my mind,
And will acknowledge you and Jessica
In place of Lord Bassanio and myself.
So fare you well, till we shall meet again.

LORENZO.

Fair thoughts and happy hours attend on you!

JESSICA.

I wish your ladyship all heart's content.

PORTIA.

I thank you for your wish, and am well pleased
To wish it back on you: fare you well, Jessica.

                        [*Exeunt* JESSICA *and* LORENZO.

Now, Balthazar,
As I have ever found thee honest-true,
So let me find thee still. Take this same letter,
And use thou all the endeavour of a man
In speed to Padua: see thou render this
Into my cousin's hand, Doctor Bellario;
And, look, what notes and garments he doth give thee,
Bring them, I pray thee, with imagined speed
Unto the traject, to the common ferry
Which trades to Venice. Waste no time in words,
But get thee gone: I shall be there before thee.

BALTHAZAR.
Madam, I go with all convenient speed.

                                        [*Exit.*

PORTIA.
Come on, Nerissa; I have work in hand
That you yet know not of: we'll see our husbands
Before they think of us.

NERISSA.
                         Shall they see us?

PORTIA.
They shall, Nerissa; but in such a habit,
That they shall think we are accomplished
With that we lack. I'll hold thee any wager,
When we are both accoutred like young men,
I'll prove the prettier fellow of the two,
And wear my dagger with the braver grace;
And speak between the change of man and boy
With a reed voice; and turn two mincing steps

Into a manly stride; and speak of frays,
Like a fine-bragging youth; and tell quaint
lies,
How honourable ladies sought my love,
Which I denying, they fell sick and died, —
I could not do withal; — then I'll repent,
And wish, for all that, that I had not kill'd
them:
And twenty of these puny lies I'll tell;
That men shall swear I have discontinued
school
Above a twelvemonth: — I have within my
mind
A thousand raw tricks of these bragging Jacks,
Which I will practise.

NERISSA.
                    Why, shall we turn to men?
PORTIA.
Fie, what a question's that,
If thou wert near a lewd interpreter!
But come, I'll tell thee all my whole device
When I am in my coach, which stays for us
At the park-gate; and therefore haste away,
For we must measure twenty miles today.
                                        [*Exeunt.*

Scene V.

The same. A garden.
Enter LAUNCELOT *and* JESSICA.

LAUNCELOT.

Yes, truly; for, look you, the sins of the father are to be laid upon the children: therefore, I promise ye, I fear you. I was always plain with you, and so now I speak my agitation of the matter: therefore be o' good cheer; for, truly, I think you are damn'd. There is but one hope in it that can do you any good; and that is but a kind of bastard hope neither.

JESSICA.

And what hope is that, I pray thee?

LAUNCELOT.

Marry, you may partly hope that your father got you not, – that you are not the Jew's daughter.

JESSICA.

That were a kind of bastard hope, indeed: so the sins of my mother should be visited upon me.

LAUNCELOT.

Truly, then, I fear you are damn'd both by father and mother: thus when I shun Scylla,

101

your father, I fall into Charybdis, your mother:
well, you are gone both ways.

JESSICA.

I shall be saved by my husband; he hath
made me a Christian.

LAUNCELOT.

Truly, the more to blame he: we were Christians
enow before; e'en as many as could well live,
one by another. This making of Christians
will raise the price of hogs: if we grow all
to be pork-eaters, we shall not shortly have
a rasher on the coals for money.

JESSICA.

I'll tell my husband, Launcelot, what you say:
here he comes.

Enter LORENZO.

LORENZO.

I shall grow jealous of you shortly, Launcelot,
if you thus get my wife into corners.

JESSICA.

Nay, you need not fear us, Lorenzo: Launcelot
and I are out. He tells me flatly, there's no
mercy for me in heaven, because I am a
Jew's daughter: and he says, you are no
good member of the commonwealth; for, in
converting Jews to Christians, you raise the
price of pork.

LORENZO.

I shall answer that better to the commonwealth
than you can the getting up of the negro's belly:

the Moor's with child by you, Launcelot.

LAUNCELOT.

It is much that the Moor should be more than reason: but if she be less than an honest woman, she is indeed more than I took her for.

LORENZO.

How every fool can play upon the word! I think the best grace of wit will shortly turn into silence, and discourse grow commendable in none only but parrots. – Go in, sirrah; bid them prepare for dinner.

LAUNCELOT.

That's done, sir; they have all stomachs.

LORENZO.

Goodly Lord, what a wit-snapper are you! then bid them prepare dinner.

LAUNCELOT.

That is done too, sir; only 'cover' is the word.

LORENZO.

Will you cover, then, sir?

LAUNCELOT.

Not so, sir, neither; I know my duty.

LORENZO.

Yet more quarrelling with occasion! Wilt thou show the whole wealth of thy wit in an instant? I pray thee, understand a plain man in his plain meaning: go to thy fellows, bid them cover the table, serve in the meat, and we will come in to dinner.

LAUNCELOT.

For the table, sir, it shall be served in; for

the meat, sir, it shall be cover'd; for your
coming in to dinner, sir, why, let it be as
humours and conceits shall govern.

[*Exit.*

LORENZO.

O dear discretion, how his words are suited!
The fool hath planted in his memory
An army of good words; and I do know
A many fools, that stand in better place,
Garnish'd like him, that for a tricksy word
Defy the matter. – How cheer'st thou, Jessica?
And now, good sweet, say thy opinion, –
How dost thou like the Lord Bassanio's wife?

JESSICA.

Past all expressing. It is very meet
The Lord Bassanio live an upright life;
For, having such a blessing in his lady,
He finds the joys of heaven here on earth;
And if on earth he do not mean it, then
In reason he should never come to heaven.
Why, if two gods should play some heavenly
match,
And on the wager lay two earthly women,
And Portia one, there must be something else
Pawn'd with the other; for the poor rude
world
Hath not her fellow.

LORENZO.

Even such a husband
Hast thou of me as she is for a wife.

JESSICA.

Nay, but ask my opinion too of that.

LORENZO.
I will anon: first, let us go to dinner.
JESSICA.
Nay, let me praise you while I have a stomach.
LORENZO.
No, prithee, let it serve for table-talk;
Then, howsoe'er thou speak'st, 'mong other things
I shall digest it.
JESSICA.
                    Well, I'll set you forth.
                                    [*Exeunt.*

ACT IV

Scene I.

Venice. A court of justice.
Enter the DUKE, *the* MAGNIFICOES, ANTONIO,
BASSANIO, GRATIANO, SOLANIO, SALARINO,
and others.

DUKE OF VENICE.
What, is Antonio here?

ANTONIO.
Ready, so please your Grace.

DUKE OF VENICE.
I am sorry for thee: thou art come to answer
A stony adversary, an inhuman wretch
Uncapable of pity, void and empty
From any dram of mercy.

ANTONIO.
                I have heard
Your Grace hath ta'en great pains to qualify
His rigorous course; but since he stands obdurate,
And that no lawful means can carry me
Out of his envy's reach, I do oppose
My patience to his fury; and am arm'd
To suffer, with a quietness of spirit,
The very tyranny and rage of his.

DUKE OF VENICE.
Go one, and call the Jew into the court.

SOLANIO.
　He's ready at the door: he comes, my lord.

Enter SHYLOCK.

DUKE OF VENICE.
　Make room, and let him stand before our
　face. —
　Shylock, the world thinks, and I think so too,
　That thou but lead'st this fashion of thy malice
　To the last hour of act; and then 'tis thought
　Thou'lt show thy mercy and remorse more
　strange
　Than is thy strange apparent cruelty;
　And where thou now exact'st the penalty, —
　Which is a pound of this poor merchant's
　flesh, —
　Thou wilt not only loose the forfeiture,
　But, touch'd with human gentleness and love,
　Forgive a moiety of the principal;
　Glancing an eye of pity on his losses,
　That have of late so huddled on his back,
　Enow to press a royal merchant down,
　And pluck commiseration of his state
　From brassy bosoms and rough hearts of flint,
　From stubborn Turks and Tartars, never train'd
　To offices of tender courtesy.
　We all expect a gentle answer, Jew.
SHYLOCK.
　I have possess'd your Grace of what I purpose;
　And by our holy Sabbath have I sworn
　To have the due and forfeit of my bond:

If you deny it, let the danger light
Upon your charter and your city's freedom.
You'll ask me, why I rather choose to have
A weight of carrion-flesh than to receive
Three thousand ducats: I'll not answer that;
But say it is my humour: is it answer'd?
What if my house be troubled with a rat,
And I be pleased to give ten thousand ducats
To have it baned! What, are you answer'd yet?
Some men there are love not a gaping pig;
Some, that are mad if they behold a cat;
And others, when the bag-pipe sings i' th'
nose,
Cannot contain their urine: for affection,
Mistress of passion, sways it to the mood
Of what it likes or loathes. Now, for your
answer:
As there is no firm reason to be render'd,
Why he cannot abide a gaping pig;
Why he, a harmless necessary cat;
Why he, a woollen bag-pipe, — but of force
Must yield to such inevitable shame
As to offend himself, being offended;
So can I give no reason, nor I will not,
More than a lodged hate and a certain loathing
I bear Antonio, that I follow thus
A losing suit against him. Are you answer'd?
BASSANIO.
This is no answer, thou unfeeling man,
To excuse the current of thy cruelty.
SHYLOCK.
I am not bound to please thee with my answer.

BASSANIO.

Do all men kill the things they do not love?

SHYLOCK.

Hates any man the thing he would not kill?

BASSANIO.

Every offence is not a hate at first.

SHYLOCK.

What, would'st thou have a serpent sting thee twice?

ANTONIO.

I pray you, think you question with the Jew:
You may as well go stand upon the beach,
And bid the main flood bate his usual height;
You may as well use question with the wolf,
Why he hath made the ewe bleat for the lamb;
You may as well forbid the mountain pines
To wag their high tops, and to make no noise,
When they are fretten with the gusts of heaven;
You may as well do any thing most hard,
As seek to soften that, — than which what's harder? —
His Jewish heart: — therefore, I do beseech you,
Make no more offers, use no further means,
But, with all brief and plain conveniency,
Let me have judgement, and the Jew his will.

BASSANIO.

For thy three thousand ducats here is six.

SHYLOCK.

If every ducat in six thousand ducats
Were in six parts, and every part a ducat,

I would not draw them, — I would have my
bond.

DUKE OF VENICE.

How shalt thou hope for mercy, rendering
none?

SHYLOCK.

What judgement shall I dread, doing no wrong?
You have among you many a purchased slave,
Which, like your asses and your dogs and
mules
You use in abject and in slavish parts,
Because you bought them: — shall I say to
you,
Let them be free, marry them to your heirs?
Why sweat they under burdens? let their beds
Be made as soft as yours, and let their palates
Be season'd with such viands? You will answer,
The slaves are ours: — so do I answer you:
The pound of flesh, which I demand of him,
Is dearly bought, 'tis mine, and I will have it.
If you deny me, fie upon your law!
There is no force in the decrees of Venice.
I stand for judgment: answer, — shall I have it?

DUKE OF VENICE.

Upon my power I may dismiss this court,
Unless Bellario, a learned doctor,
Whom I have sent for to determine this,
Come here today.

SOLANIO.

　　　　　　　My lord, here stays without
A messenger with letters from the doctor,
New come from Padua.

DUKE OF VENICE.

Bring us the letters; call the messenger.

BASSANIO.

Good cheer, Antonio! What, man, courage yet!
The Jew shall have my flesh, blood, bones, and
all,
Ere thou shalt lose for me one drop of blood.

ANTONIO.

I am a tainted wether of the flock,
Meetest for death: the weakest kind of fruit
Drops earliest to the ground; and so let me:
You cannot better be employ'd, Bassanio,
Than to live still, and write mine epitaph.

Enter NERISSA, *dressed like a lawyer's clerk.*

DUKE OF VENICE.

Came you from Padua, from Bellario?

NERISSA.

From both, my lord. Bellario greets your
Grace.

[*Presents a letter.*

BASSANIO.

Why dost thou whet thy knife so earnestly?

SHYLOCK.

To cut the forfeiture from that bankrupt there.

GRATIANO.

Not on thy sole, but on thy soul, harsh Jew,
Thou makest thy knife keen; but no metal can,
No, not the hangman's axe, bear half the
keenness
Of thy sharp envy. Can no prayers pierce thee?

SHYLOCK.
No, none that thou hast wit enough to make.
GRATIANO.
O, be thou damn'd, inexecrable dog!
And for thy life let justice be accused.
Thou almost makest me waver in my faith,
To hold opinion with Pythagoras,
That souls of animals infuse themselves
Into the trunks of men: thy currish spirit
Govern'd a wolf, who, hang'd for human slaughter,
Even from the gallows did his fell soul fleet,
And, whilst thou lay'st in thy unhallow'd dam,
Infused itself in thee; for thy desires
Are wolvish, bloody, starved, and ravenous.
SHYLOCK.
Till thou canst rail the seal from off my bond,
Thou but offend'st thy lungs to speak so loud:
Repair thy wit, good youth, or it will fall
To cureless ruin. — I stand here for law.
DUKE OF VENICE.
This letter from Bellario doth commend
A young and learned doctor to our court. —
Where is he?
NERISSA.
                    He attendeth here hard by,
To know your answer, whether you'll admit him.
DUKE OF VENICE.
With all my heart. — Some three or four of you
Go give him courteous conduct to this place. —

Meantime the court shall hear Bellario's letter.
CLERK [*reads*].

Your Grace shall understand, that at the receipt
of your letter I am very sick: but in the instant
that your messenger came, in loving visitation
was with me a young doctor of Rome; his name
is Balthazar. I acquainted him with the cause in
controversy between the Jew and Antonio the
merchant: we turn'd o'er many books together:
he is furnish'd with my opinion; which, better'd
with his own learning, — the greatness whereof
I cannot enough commend, — comes with him,
at my importunity, to fill up your Grace's
request in my stead. I beseech you, let his
lack of years be no impediment to let him
lack a reverend estimation; for I never knew
so young a body with so old a head. I leave
him to your gracious acceptance, whose trial
shall better publish his commendation.
DUKE OF VENICE.

You hear the learn'd Bellario, what he writes:
And here, I take it, is the doctor come.

Enter PORTIA *for* BALTHAZAR.

Give me your hand. Come you from old
Bellario?
PORTIA.

I did, my lord.
DUKE OF VENICE.

You are welcome: take your place.
Are you acquainted with the difference

116

That holds this present question in the court?
PORTIA.
I am informed throughly of the cause. —
Which is the merchant here, and which the
Jew?
DUKE OF VENICE.
Antonio and old Shylock, both stand forth.
PORTIA.
Is your name Shylock?
SHYLOCK.

                        Shylock is my name.
PORTIA.
Of a strange nature is the suit you follow;
Yet in such rule, that the Venetian law
Cannot impugn you as you do proceed. —
You stand within his danger, do you not?
ANTONIO.
Ay, so he says.
PORTIA.

                      Do you confess the bond?
ANTONIO.
I do.
PORTIA.

                    Then must the Jew be merciful.
SHYLOCK.
On what compulsion must I? tell me that.
PORTIA.
The quality of mercy is not strain'd, —
It droppeth as the gentle rain from heaven
Upon the place beneath: it is twice blest, —
It blesseth him that gives, and him that takes:
'Tis mightiest in the mightiest: it becomes

117

The throned monarch better than his crown;
His sceptre shows the force of temporal power,
The attribute to awe and majesty,
Wherein doth sit the dread and fear of kings;
But mercy is above this sceptred sway, —
It is enthroned in the hearts of kings,
It is an attribute to God himself;
And earthly power doth then show likest
God's
When mercy seasons justice. Therefore, Jew,
Though justice be thy plea, consider this, —
That, in the course of justice, none of us
Should see salvation: we do pray for mercy;
And that same prayer doth teach us all to
render
The deeds of mercy. I have spoke thus much
To mitigate the justice of thy plea;
Which if thou follow, this strict court of
Venice
Must needs give sentence 'gainst the merchant
there.

SHYLOCK.
My deeds upon my head! I crave the law,
The penalty and forfeit of my bond.

PORTIA.
Is he not able to discharge the money?

BASSANIO.
Yes, here I tender it for him in the court;
Yea, thrice the sum: if that will not suffice,
I will be bound to pay it ten times o'er,
On forfeit of my hands, my head, my heart:
If this will not suffice, it must appear

That malice bears down truth. And I beseech
you,
Wrest once the law to your authority:
To do a great right, do a little wrong;
And curb this cruel devil of his will.

PORTIA.
It must not be; there is no power in Venice
Can alter a decree established:
'Twill be recorded for a precedent;
And many an error, by the same example,
Will rush into the state: it cannot be.

SHYLOCK.
A Daniel come to judgement! yea, a Daniel! —
O wise young judge, how I do honour thee!

PORTIA.
I pray you, let me look upon the bond.

SHYLOCK.
Here 'tis, most reverend doctor, here it is.

PORTIA.
Shylock, there's thrice thy money offer'd thee.

SHYLOCK.
An oath, an oath, I have an oath in heaven:
Shall I lay perjury upon my soul?
No, not for Venice.

PORTIA.
                    Why, this bond is forfeit;
And lawfully by this the Jew may claim
A pound of flesh, to be by him cut off
Nearest the merchant's heart. — Be merciful:
Take thrice thy money; bid me tear the bond.

SHYLOCK.
When it is paid according to the tenour. —

It doth appear you are a worthy judge;
You know the law, your exposition
Hath been most sound: I charge you by the law,
Whereof you are a well-deserving pillar,
Proceed to judgement: by my soul I swear
There is no power in the tongue of man
To alter me: I stay here on my bond.

ANTONIO.
Most heartily I do beseech the court
To give the judgement.

PORTIA.
                        Why then, thus it is: —
You must prepare your bosom for his knife.

SHYLOCK.
O noble judge! O excellent young man!

PORTIA.
For the intent and purpose of the law
Hath full relation to the penalty,
Which here appeareth due upon the bond.

SHYLOCK.
'Tis very true: O wise and upright judge!
How much more elder art thou than thy looks!

PORTIA.
Therefore lay bare your bosom.

SHYLOCK.
                        Ay, his breast:
So says the bond: — doth it not, noble judge? —
Nearest his heart: those are the very words.

PORTIA.
It is so. Are there balance here to weigh
The flesh?

SHYLOCK.

I have them ready.

PORTIA.

Have by some surgeon, Shylock, on your charge,

To stop his wounds, lest he do bleed to death.

SHYLOCK.

Is it so nominated in the bond?

PORTIA.

It is not so express'd: but what of that?

'Twere good you do so much for charity.

SHYLOCK.

I cannot find it; 'tis not in the bond.

PORTIA.

You, merchant, have you any thing to say?

ANTONIO.

But little: I am arm'd and well prepared. —

Give me your hand, Bassanio: fare you well!

Grieve not that I am fall'n to this for you;

For herein Fortune shows herself more kind

Than is her custom: it is still her use

To let the wretched man outlive his wealth,

To view with hollow eye and wrinkled brow

An age of poverty; from which lingering penance

Of such a misery doth she cut me off.

Commend me to your honourable wife:

Tell her the process of Antonio's end;

Say how I loved you, speak me fair in death;

And, when the tale is told, bid her be judge

Whether Bassanio had not once a love.

Repent but you that you shall lose your friend,

121

And he repents not that he pays your debt;
For, if the Jew do cut but deep enough,
I'll pay it presently with all my heart.

BASSANIO.

Antonio, I am married to a wife
Which is as dear to me as life itself;
But life itself, my wife, and all the world,
Are not with me esteem'd above thy life:
I would lose all, ay, sacrifice them all
Here to this devil, to deliver you.

PORTIA.

Your wife would give you little thanks for that,
If she were by, to hear you make the offer.

GRATIANO.

I have a wife, whom, I protest, I love:
I would she were in heaven, so she could
Entreat some power to change this currish Jew.

NERISSA.

'Tis well you offer it behind her back;
The wish would make else an unquiet house.

SHYLOCK [*aside*].

These be the Christian husbands! I have a
daughter;
Would any of the stock of Barabbas
Had been her husband rather than a Christian! —
We trifle time: I pray thee, pursue sentence.

PORTIA.

A pound of that same merchant's flesh is
thine:
The court awards it, and the law doth give it.

SHYLOCK.

Most rightful judge!

PORTIA.

And you must cut this flesh from off his breast:

The law allows it, and the court awards it.

SHYLOCK.

Most learned judge! — A sentence! come, pre-pare!

PORTIA.

Tarry a little; there is something else.

This bond doth give thee here no jot of blood, —

The words expressly are, 'a pound of flesh':

Take then thy bond, take thou thy pound of flesh;

But, in the cutting it, if thou dost shed

One drop of Christian blood, thy lands and goods

Are, by the laws of Venice, confiscate

Unto the state of Venice.

GRATIANO.

O upright judge! — Mark, Jew: — O learned judge!

SHYLOCK.

Is that the law?

PORTIA.

Thyself shalt see the act:

For, as thou urgest justice, be assured

Thou shalt have justice, more than thou desirest.

GRATIANO.

O learned judge! — Mark, Jew: — a learned judge!

SHYLOCK.

I take his offer, then; — pay the bond thrice,
And let the Christian go.

BASSANIO.

Here is the money.

PORTIA.

Soft!
The Jew shall have all justice; — soft! no
haste: —
He shall have nothing but the penalty.

GRATIANO.

O Jew! an upright judge, a learned judge!

PORTIA.

Therefore prepare thee to cut off the flesh.
Shed thou no blood; nor cut thou less nor
more
But just a pound of flesh: if thou cutt'st more
Or less than a just pound, — be it but so much
As makes it light or heavy in the substance,
Or the division of the twentieth part
Of one poor scruple, nay, if the scale do turn
But in the estimation of a hair, —
Thou diest, and all thy goods are confiscate.

GRATIANO.

A second Daniel, a Daniel, Jew!
Now, infidel, I have you on the hip.

PORTIA.

Why doth the Jew pause? take thy forfeiture.

SHYLOCK.

Give me my principal, and let me go.

BASSANIO.

I have it ready for thee; here it is.

PORTIA.

He hath refused it in the open court:

He shall have merely justice and his bond.

GRATIANO.

A Daniel, still say I, a second Daniel! —

I thank thee, Jew, for teaching me that word.

SHYLOCK.

Shall I not have barely my principal?

PORTIA.

Thou shalt have nothing but the forfeiture,

To be so taken at thy peril, Jew.

SHYLOCK.

Why, then the devil give him good of it!

I'll stay no longer question.

PORTIA.

Tarry, Jew:

The law hath yet another hold on you.

It is enacted in the laws of Venice, —

If it be proved against an alien

That by direct or indirect attempts

He seek the life of any citizen,

The party 'gainst the which he doth contrive

Shall seize one half his goods; the other half

Comes to the privy coffer of the state;

And the offender's life lies in the mercy

Of the duke only, 'gainst all other voice.

In which predicament, I say, thou stand'st;

For it appears, by manifest proceeding,

That indirectly, and directly too,

Thou hast contrived against the very life

Of the defendant; and thou hast incurr'd

The danger formerly by me rehearsed.

Down, therefore, and beg mercy of the duke.

GRATIANO.

Beg that thou mayst have leave to hang
thyself:
And yet, thy wealth being forfeit to the state,
Thou hast not left the value of a cord;
Therefore thou must be hang'd at the state's
charge.

DUKE OF VENICE.

That thou shalt see the difference of our spirits,
I pardon thee thy life before thou ask it:
For half thy wealth, it is Antonio's;
The other half comes to the general state,
Which humbleness may drive unto a fine.

PORTIA.

Ay, for the state, — not for Antonio.

SHYLOCK.

Nay, take my life and all; pardon not that:
You take my house, when you do take the prop
That doth sustain my house; you take my life,
When you do take the means whereby I live.

PORTIA.

What mercy can you render him, Antonio?

GRATIANO.

A halter gratis; nothing else, for God's sake.

ANTONIO.

So please my lord the duke and all the court
To quit the fine for one half of his goods,
I am content; so he will let me have
The other half in use, to render it,
Upon his death, unto the gentleman
That lately stole his daughter:

Two things provided more, — that, for this
favour,
He presently become a Christian;
The other, that he do record a gift,
Here in the court, of all he dies possess'd,
Unto his son Lorenzo and his daughter.

DUKE OF VENICE.
He shall do this; or else I do recant
The pardon that I late pronounced here.

PORTIA.
Art thou contented, Jew? what dost thou say?

SHYLOCK.
I am content.

PORTIA.
                         Clerk, draw a deed of gift.

SHYLOCK.
I pray you, give me leave to go from hence;
I am not well: send the deed after me,
And I will sign it.

DUKE OF VENICE.
                    Get thee gone, but do it.

GRATIANO.
In christening shalt thou have two godfathers:
Had I been judge, thou shouldst have had ten
more,
To bring thee to the gallows, not the font.
                              [*Exit* SHYLOCK.

DUKE OF VENICE.
Sir, I entreat you home with me to dinner.

PORTIA.
I humbly do desire your Grace of pardon:
I must away this night toward Padua,

And it is meet I presently set forth.
DUKE OF VENICE.
  I am sorry that your leisure serves you not. —
  Antonio, gratify this gentleman;
  For, in my mind, you are much bound to him.
                      [*Exeunt* DUKE *and his* TRAIN.
BASSANIO.
  Most worthy gentleman, I and my friend
  Have by your wisdom been this day acquitted
  Of grievous penalties; in lieu whereof
  Three thousand ducats, due unto the Jew,
  We freely cope your courteous pains withal.
ANTONIO.
  And stand indebted, over and above,
  In love and service to you evermore.
PORTIA.
  He is well paid that is well satisfied;
  And I, delivering you, am satisfied,
  And therein do account myself well paid:
  My mind was never yet more mercenary.
  I pray you, know me when we meet again:
  I wish you well, and so I take my leave.
BASSANIO.
  Dear sir, of force I must attempt you further:
  Take some remembrance of us, as a tribute,
  Not as a fee: grant me two things, I pray
  you, —
  Not to deny me, and to pardon me.
PORTIA.
  You press me far, and therefore I will yield.
  [*to* ANTONIO] Give me your gloves, I'll wear
  them for your sake;

[*to* BASSANIO] And, for your love, I'll take this
ring from you: —
Do not draw back your hand; I'll take no
more;
And you in love shall not deny me this.

BASSANIO.
This ring, good sir, — alas, it is trifle!
I will not shame myself to give you this.

PORTIA.
I will have nothing else but only this;
And now methinks I have a mind to it.

BASSANIO.
There's more depends on this than on the
value,
The dearest ring in Venice will I give you,
And find it out by proclamation:
Only for this, I pray you, pardon me.

PORTIA.
I see, sir, you are liberal in offers:
You taught me first to beg; and now methinks
You teach me how a beggar should be answer'd.

BASSANIO.
Good sir, this ring was given me by my wife;
And, when she put it on, she made me vow
That I should neither sell nor give nor lose it.

PORTIA.
That 'scuse serves many men to save their
gifts.
An if your wife be not a mad-woman,
And know how well I have deserved this ring,
She would not hold out enemy for ever
For giving it to me. Well, peace be with you!

> [*Exeunt* PORTIA *and* NERISSA.

ANTONIO.

My Lord Bassanio, let him have the ring:
Let his deservings, and my love withal,
Be valued 'gainst your wife's commandment.

BASSANIO.

Go, Gratiano, run and overtake him;
Give him this ring; and bring him, if thou canst,
Unto Antonio's house: — away! make haste.

> [*Exit* GRATIANO.

Come, you and I will thither presently;
And in the morning early will be both
Fly toward Belmont: come, Antonio.

> [*Exeunt.*

Scene II.

The same. A street.
Enter PORTIA *and* NERISSA.

PORTIA.
> Inquire the Jew's house out, give him this
> deed,
> And let him sign it. we'll away tonight,
> And be a day before our husbands home:
> This deed will be well welcome to Lorenzo.

Enter GRATIANO.

GRATIANO.
> Fair sir, you are well o'erta'en:
> My Lord Bassanio, upon more advice,
> Hath sent you here this ring; and doth entreat
> Your company at dinner.

PORTIA.
>   That cannot be:
> His ring I do accept most thankfully;
> And so, I pray you, tell him: furthermore,
> I pray you, show my youth old Shylock's
> house.

GRATIANO.
> That will I do.

131

NERISSA.

        Sir, I would speak with you. —
[*to* PORTIA] I'll see if I can get my husband's
ring,
Which I did make him swear to keep for ever.
PORTIA [*to* NERISSA].
Thou mayst, I warrant. We shall have old
swearing
That they did give the rings away to men;
But we'll outface them, and outswear them
too. —
Away! make haste: thou know'st where I will
tarry.
NERISSA.
Come, good sir, will you show me to this
house?

                          [*Exeunt.*

ACT V

Scene I.

Belmont. Avenue to PORTIA'S house.
Enter LORENZO *and* JESSICA.

LORENZO.
    The moon shines bright: — in such a night as
    this,
    When the sweet wind did gently kiss the trees,
    And they did make no noise, — in such a
    night
    Troilus methinks mounted the Troyan walls,
    And sigh'd his soul toward the Grecian tents,
    Where Cressid lay that night.
JESSICA.
                            In such a night
    Did Thisbe fearfully o'ertrip the dew,
    And saw the lion's shadow ere himself,
    And ran dismay'd away.
LORENZO.
                            In such a night
    Stood Dido with a willow in her hand
    Upon the wild sea-banks, and waft her love
    To come again to Carthage.
JESSICA.
                            In such a night
    Medea gather'd the enchanted herbs
    That did renew old Aeson.

LORENZO.

                    In such a night
Did Jessica steal from the wealthy Jew,
And with an unthrift love did run from Venice
As far as Belmont.

JESSICA.

                    In such a night
Did young Lorenzo swear he loved her well,
Stealing her soul with many vows of faith,
And ne'er a true one.

LORENZO.

                    In such a night
Did pretty Jessica, like a little shrew,
Slander her love, and he forgave it her.

JESSICA.

I would out-night you, did no body come:
But, hark, I hear the footing of a man.

Enter STEPHANO.

LORENZO.

Who comes so fast in silence of the night?

STEPHANO.

A friend.

LORENZO.

A friend! what friend? your name, I pray you,
friend?

STEPHANO.

Stephano is my name; and I bring word
My mistress will before the break of day
Be here at Belmont: she doth stray about
By holy crosses, where she kneels and prays

For happy wedlock hours.

LORENZO.

Who comes with her?

STEPHANO.

None but a holy hermit and her maid.
I pray you, is my master yet return'd?

LORENZO.

He is not, nor we have not heard from him. —
But go we in, I pray thee, Jessica,
And ceremoniously let us prepare
Some welcome for the mistress of the house.

Enter LAUNCELOT.

LAUNCELOT GOBBO.

Sola, sola! wo ha, ho! sola, sola!

LORENZO.

Who calls?

LAUNCELOT GOBBO.

Sola! — did you see Master Lorenzo? Master
Lorenzo! — sola, sola!

LORENZO.

Leave hollaing, man: — here.

LAUNCELOT GOBBO.

Sola! — where? where?

LORENZO.

Here.

LAUNCELOT GOBBO.

Tell him there's a post come from my master,
with his horn full of good news: my master
will be here ere morning.

[*Exit.*

137

LORENZO.
   Sweet soul, let's in, and there expect their
coming.
   And yet no matter: — why should we go in? —
My friend Stephano, signify, I pray you,
Within the house, your mistress is at hand;
And bring your music forth into the air.
                                    [*Exit* STEPHANO.
How sweet the moonlight sleeps upon this bank!
Here will we sit, and let the sounds of music
Creep in our ears: soft stillness and the night
Become the touches of sweet harmony.
Sit, Jessica. Look, how the floor of heaven
Is thick inlaid with patines of bright gold:
There's not the smallest orb which thou behold'st
But in his motion like an angel sings,
Still quiring to the young-eyed cherubins, —
Such harmony is in immortal souls;
But whilst this muddy vesture of decay
Doth grossly close it in, we cannot hear it.

                    Enter MUSICIANS.

Come, ho, and wake Diana with a hymn!
With sweetest touches pierce your mistress' ear,
And draw her home with music.
                                    [*Music plays.*
JESSICA.
   I am never merry when I hear sweet music.
LORENZO.
   The reason is, your spirits are attentive:
For do but note a wild and wanton herd,

Or race of youthful and unhandled colts,
Fetching mad bounds, bellowing, and neighing
loud,
Which is the hot condition of their blood;
If they but hear perchance a trumpet sound,
Or any air of music touch their ears,
You shall perceive them make a mutual stand,
Their savage eyes turn'd to a modest gaze,
By the sweet power of music: therefore the poet
Did feign that Orpheus drew trees, stones, and
floods;
Since naught so stockish, hard, and full of rage,
But music for the time doth change his nature.
The man that hath no music in himself,
Nor is not moved with concord of sweet sounds,
Is fit for treasons, stratagems, and spoils;
The motions of his spirit are dull as night,
And his affections dark as Erebus:
Let no such man be trusted. — Mark the music.

Enter PORTIA *and* NERISSA.

PORTIA.
That light we see is burning in my hall.
How far that little candle throws his beams!
So shines a good deed in a naughty world.
NERISSA.
When the moon shone, we did not see the
candle.
PORTIA.
So doth the greater glory dim the less:
A substitute shines brightly as a king,

Until a king be by; and then his state
Empties itself, as doth an inland brook
Into the main of waters. — Music! hark!
NERISSA.
It is your music, madam, of the house.
PORTIA.
Nothing is good, I see, without respect:
Methinks it sounds much sweeter than by day.
NERISSA.
Silence bestows that virtue on it, madam.
PORTIA.
The crow doth sing as sweetly as the lark,
When neither is attended; and I think
The nightingale, if she should sing by day,
When every goose is cackling, would be thought
No better a musician than the wren.
How many things by season season'd are
To their right praise and true perfection! —
Peace, ho! the moon sleeps with Endymion,
And would not be awaked.

[*Music ceases.*

LORENZO.

That is the voice,
Or I am much deceived, of Portia.
PORTIA.
He knows me, as the blind man knows the cuckoo,
By the bad voice.
LORENZO.

Dear lady, welcome home.
PORTIA.
We have been praying for our husband's health,

Which speed, we hope, the better for our words.
Are they return'd?
LORENZO.

             Madam, they are not yet;
But there is come a messenger before,
To signify their coming.
PORTIA.

            Go in, Nerissa;
Give orders to my servants that they take
No note at all of our being absent hence; —
Nor you, Lorenzo; — Jessica, nor you.

                     [*A tucket sounds.*

LORENZO.
Your husband is at hand; I hear his trumpet:
We are no tell-tales, madam; fear you not.
PORTIA.
This night methinks is but the daylight sick;
It looks a little paler: 'tis a day,
Such as the day is when the sun is hid.

      Enter BASSANIO, ANTONIO, GRATIANO,
         and their FOLLOWERS.

BASSANIO.
We should hold day with the Antipodes,
If you would walk in absence of the sun.
PORTIA.
Let me give light, but let me not be light;
For a light wife doth make a heavy husband,
And never be Bassanio so for me:
But God sort all! — You're welcome home, my
lord.

BASSANIO.
   I thank you, madam. Give welcome to my
   friend:
   This is the man, this is Antonio,
   To whom I am so infinitely bound.
PORTIA.
   You should in all sense be much bound to him,
   For, as I hear, he was much bound for you.
ANTONIO.
   No more than I am well acquitted of.
PORTIA.
   Sir, you are very welcome to our house:
   It must appear in other ways than words,
   Therefore I scant this breathing courtesy.
GRATIANO [to NERISSA].
   By yonder moon I swear you do me wrong;
   In faith, I gave it to the judge's clerk:
   Would he were gelt that had it, for my part,
   Since you do take it, love, so much at heart.
PORTIA.
   A quarrel, ho, already! what's the matter?
GRATIANO.
   About a hoop of gold, a paltry ring
   That she did give to me; whose posy was
   For all the world like cutler's poetry
   Upon a knife, 'Love me, and leave me not.'
NERISSA.
   What talk you of the posy or the value?
   You swore to me, when I did give it you,
   That you would wear it till your hour of death;
   And that it should lie with you in your grave:
   Though not for me, yet for your vehement oaths,

You should have been respective, and have kept
it.
Gave it a judge's clerk! no, God's my judge,
The clerk will ne'er wear hair on's face that had
it.

GRATIANO.
He will, an if he live to be a man.

NERISSA.
Ay, if a woman live to be a man.

GRATIANO.
Now, by this hand, I gave it to a youth, —
A kind of boy; a little scrubbed boy,
No higher than thyself, the judge's clerk;
A prating boy, that begg'd it as a fee:
I could not for my heart deny it him.

PORTIA.
You were to blame, — I must be plain with
you, —
To part so slightly with your wife's first gift;
A thing stuck on with oaths upon your finger,
And so riveted with faith unto your flesh.
I gave my love a ring, and made him swear
Never to part with it; and here he stands, —
I dare be sworn for him, he would not leave
it,
Nor pluck it from his finger, for the wealth
That the world masters. Now, in faith, Gratiano,
You give your wife too unkind a cause of grief:
An'twere to me, I should be mad at it.

BASSANIO [aside].
Why, I were best to cut my left hand off,
And swear I lost the ring defending it.

GRATIANO.

    My Lord Bassanio gave his ring away
Unto the judge that begg'd it, and indeed
Deserved it too; and then the boy, his clerk,
That took some pains in writing, he begg'd
mine:
And neither man nor master would take aught
But the two rings.

PORTIA.

                What ring gave you, my lord?
Not that, I hope, which you received of me.

BASSANIO.

    If I could add a lie unto a fault,
I would deny it; but you see my finger
Hath not the ring upon it, — it is gone.

PORTIA.

    Even so void is your false heart of truth.
By heaven, I will ne'er come in your bed
Until I see the ring.

NERISSA.

                Nor I in yours
Till I again see mine.

BASSANIO.

                Sweet Portia,
If you did know to whom I gave the ring,
If you did know for whom I gave the ring,
And would conceive for what I gave the ring,
And how unwillingly I left the ring,
When naught would be accepted but the ring,
You would abate the strength of your displeasure.

PORTIA.

    If you had known the virtue of the ring,

Or half her worthiness that gave the ring,
Or your own honour to contain the ring,
You would not then have parted with the ring.
What man is there so much unreasonable,
If you had pleased to have defended it
With any terms of zeal, wanted the modesty
To urge the thing held as a ceremony?
Nerissa teaches me what to believe:
I'll die for't but some woman had the ring.

BASSANIO.
No, by my honour, madam, by my soul,
No woman had it, but a civil doctor,
Which did refuse three thousand ducats of me,
And begg'd the ring; the which I did deny him,
And suffer'd him to go displeased away;
Even he that did uphold the very life
Of my dear friend. What should I say, sweet
lady?
I was enforced to send it after him:
I was beset with shame and courtesy;
My honour would not let ingratitude
So much besmear it. Pardon me, good lady;
For, by these blessed candles of the night,
Had you been there, I think, you would have
begg'd
The ring of me to give the worthy doctor.

PORTIA.
Let not that doctor e'er come near my house:
Since he hath got the jewel that I loved,
And that which you did swear to keep for me,
I will become as liberal as you;
I'll not deny him any thing I have,

No, not my body nor my husband's bed:
Know him I shall, I am well sure of it:
Lie not a night from home; watch me like
Argus:
If you do not, if I be left alone,
Now, by mine honour, which is yet mine own,
I'll have that doctor for my bedfellow.

NERISSA.

And I his clerk; therefore be well advised
How you do leave me to mine own protection.

GRATIANO.

Well, do you so: let not me take him, then;
For if I do, I'll mar the young clerk's pen.

ANTONIO.

I am the unhappy subject of these quarrels.

PORTIA.

Sir, grieve not you; you are welcome
notwithstanding.

BASSANIO.

Portia, forgive me this enforced wrong;
And, in the hearing of these many friends,
I swear to thee, even by thine own fair eyes,
Wherein I see myself, —

PORTIA.

                              Mark you but that!
In both my eyes he doubly sees himself;
In each eye, one: — swear by your double self,
And there's an oath of credit.

BASSANIO.

                              Nay, but hear me:
Pardon this fault, and by my soul I swear
I never more will break an oath with thee.

ANTONIO.

    I once did lend my body for his wealth;
    Which, but for him that had your husband's
    ring,
    Had quite miscarried: I dare be bound again,
    My soul upon the forfeit, that your lord
    Will never more break faith advisedly.

PORTIA.

    Then you shall be his surety. Give him this;
    And bid him keep it better than the other.

ANTONIO.

    Here, Lord Bassanio; swear to keep this ring.

BASSANIO.

    By heaven, it is the same I gave the doctor!

PORTIA.

    I had it of him: pardon me, Bassanio;
    For, by this ring, the doctor lay with me.

NERISSA.

    And pardon me, my gentle Gratiano;
    For that same scrubbed boy, the doctor's clerk,
    In lieu of this, last night did lie with me.

GRATIANO.

    Why, this is like the mending of highways
    In summer, where the ways are fair enough:
    What, are we cuckolds ere we have deserved it?

PORTIA.

    Speak not so grossly. — You are all amazed:
    Here is a letter, read it at your leisure;
    It comes from Padua, from Bellario:
    There you shall find that Portia was the doctor;
    Nerissa there her clerk: Lorenzo here
    Shall witness I set forth as soon as you,

And even but now return'd; I have not yet
Enter'd my house. — Antonio, you are welcome;
And I have better news in store for you
Than you expect: unseal this letter soon;
There you shall find three of your argosies
Are richly come to harbour suddenly:
You shall not know by what strange accident
I chanced on this letter.

ANTONIO.

I am dumb.

BASSANIO.

Were you the doctor, and I knew you not?

GRATIANO.

Were you the clerk that is to make me cuckold?

NERISSA.

Ay, but the clerk that never means to do it,
Unless he live until he be a man.

BASSANIO.

Sweet doctor, you shall be my bedfellow:
When I am absent, then lie with my wife.

ANTONIO.

Sweet lady, you have given me life and living;
For here I read for certain that my ships
Are safely come to road.

PORTIA.

How now, Lorenzo!
My clerk hath some good comforts too for you.

NERISSA.

Ay, and I'll give them him without a fee. —
There do I give to you and Jessica,
From the rich Jew, a special deed of gift,
After his death, of all he dies possess'd of.

LORENZO.
> Fair ladies, you drop manna in the way
> Of starved people.

PORTIA.
>   It is almost morning,
> And yet I am sure you are not satisfied
> Of these events at full. Let us go in;
> And charge us there upon inter'gatories,
> And we will answer all things faithfully.

GRATIANO.
> Let it be so: the first inter'gatory
> That my Nerissa shall be sworn on is,
> Whether till the next night she had rather stay,
> Or go to bed now, being two hours to day:
> But were the day come, I should wish it dark,
> That I were couching with the doctor's clerk.
> Well, while I live I'll fear no other thing
> So sore as keeping safe Nerissa's ring.

[Exeunt.

Glossary

ABATE: to shorten. To cast down. To blunt.

ABATEMENT: diminution.

ABIDE: to sojourn. to expiate (a corruption of 'Aby').

ABLE: to uphold.

ABRIDGEMENT: a short play.

ABROOK: to brook, abide.

ABSEY-BOOK: a primer.

ABSOLUTE: positive, certain. Complete.

ABUSE: to deceive. Deception.

ABY: to expiate a fault.

ABYSM: abyss.

ACCITE: to cite, summon.

ACCUSE: accusation.

ACHIEVE: to obtain.

ACKNOWN: 'to be acknown' is to acknowledge.

ACQUITTANCE: a receipt or discharge.

ACTION-TAKING: litigious.

ACTURE: action.

ADDITION: title, attribute.

ADDRESS: prepare oneself.

ADVANCE: to prefer, promote to honour.

ADVERTISEMENT: admonition.

ADVERTISING: attentive.

ADVICE: consideration, discretion.

ADVISE: to consider, reflect.

ADVISED: considerate.
ADVOCATION: pleading, advocacy.
AFEARED: afraid.
AFFECT: to love.
AFFEERED: assessed, confirmed.
AFFY: to affiance. To trust.
AFRONT: in front.
AGAZED: looking in amazement.
AGLET-BABY: the small figure engraved on a jewel.
AGNISE: to acknowledge, confess.
A-GOOD: a good deal, plenteously.
A-HOLD: a sea-term.
AIM: a guess.
ALDER-LIEFEST: most loved of all.
ALE: alehouse.
ALLOW: to approve.
ALLOWANCE: approval.
AMES-ACE: two aces, the lowest throw of the dice.
AMORT: dead, dejected.
AN: if.
ANCHOR: an anchorite, hermit.
ANCIENT: an ensign-bearer.
ANGEL: a coin, bearing the image of an angel.
ANIGHT: by night.
ANSWER: retaliation.
ANTHROPOPHAGINIAN: a cannibal.
ANTICK: the fool in the old plays.
ANTRE: a cave.
APPARENT: heir-apparent.
APPEAL: accusation. Accuse.

152

APPEARED: made apparent.

APPLE-JOHN: a kind of apple.

APPOINTMENT: preparation.

APPREHENSION: opinion.

APPREHENSIVE: apt to apprehend or understand.

APPROBATION: probation.

APPROOF: approbation, proof.

APPROVE: to prove. To justify, make good.

APPROVER: one who proves or tries.

ARCH: chief.

ARGAL: ergo, therefore.

ARGENTINE: silver.

ARGIER: Algiers.

ARGOSY: a merchant ship, originally of Ragusa.

ARGUMENT: subject.

ARMIGERO: Esquire.

AROINT: get thee gone.

A-ROW: in a row.

ARTICULATE: to enter into articles of agreement.

ASK: to require.

ASPECT: regard, looks.

ASPERSION: sprinkling; hence blessing, generally accompanied by the sprinkling of holy water.

ASSAY: attempt, test, make proof of.

ASSINEGO: an ass.

ASSUBJUGATE: to subjugate.

ASSURANCE: deed of assurance.

ASSURED: betrothed.

ATOMY: an atom, a small person.

ATONE: to put people at one, to reconcile.

ATTACH: to seize, lay hold on.

ATTASKED: taken to task, reprehended.

ATTEND: to listen to.

ATTENT: attentive.

ATTORNEY: an agent.

ATTORNEY: to employ as an agent. To perform by an agent.

AUDACIOUS: spirited, daring.

AUGUR: augury.

AUTHENTIC: clothed with authority.

AVAUNT: be gone, a word of abhorrence.

AVE: hail.

AVE-MARY: salutation addressed to the Blessed Virgin Mary.

AVERRING: confirming.

AWFUL: worshipful.

AWKWARD: contrary.

BACCARE: keep back.

BACKWARD: the hinder part; the past.

BALKED: heaped, as on a ridge.

BALLOW: a cudgel.

BALM: the oil of consecration.

BAN: to curse.

BANK: to sail by the banks.

BARM: yeast.

BARN: a child.

BARNACLE: a shellfish, supposed to produce the sea-bird of the same name.

BASE: a game, sometimes called Prisoners' base.

BASES: an embroidered mantle worn by knights on horseback, reaching below the knees.

BASILISK: a kind of ordnance.

BASTA: (Italian), enough.

BASTARD: raisin wine.

BATE: to flutter, as a hawk. To abate.

BAT-FOWLING: catching birds with a clap-net by night.

BATLET: a small bat, used for beating clothes.

BATTLE: army.

BAVIN: like brushwood, blazing and instantly dying.

BAWCOCK: a fine fellow.

BAY: the space between the roof timbers.

BEADSMAN: one who says prayers for another.

BEARING-CLOTH: a christening robe.

BEAT: to flutter as a falcon, to meditate, consider earnestly.

BEAVER: the lower part of a helmet.

BEETLE: a mallet.

BEING: dwelling.

BE-METE: to measure.

BE-MOILED: daubed with dirt.

BENVENUTO: (Italian), welcome.

BERGOMASK: a rustic dance.

BESHREW: evil befall; a plague upon.

BESTRAUGHT: distraught, distracted.

BETEEM: to pour out. To allow.

BETID: happened.

BEZONIAN: a beggarly fellow.

BIDING: abiding-place.

BIGGEN: a night-cap.

BILBERRY: the whortleberry.

BILBO: a sword, from Bilbao in Spain.

BILBOES: fetters or stocks.

BILL: a bill-hook, a weapon.

BIN: been, are.

BIRD-BOLT: an arrow for shooting at birds.

BIRDING: hawking at partridges.

BISSON: blind.

BLANK: the white mark in the middle of a target.

BLENCH: to start aside, flinch.

BLENT: blended.

BLOOD-BOLTERED: smeared with blood.

BLOW: to inflate.

BOARD: to accost.

BOB: a blow, or hit; a gibe. To cheat.

BODGE: to botch, bungle.

BODIKIN: 'Od's Bodikin,' God's little body.

BOITIER VERT: (French), green box.

BOLLEN: swollen.

BOLTED: sifted, refined.

BOLTER: a sieve.

BOLTING-HUTCH: a container for sifting meal.

BOMBARD: a barrel, a drunkard.

BOMBAST: padding.

BONA-ROBA: a harlot.

BOND: that to which one is bound.

BOOK: a paper of conditions.

BOOT: help, use.

BOOTS: bots, a kind of worm.

BORE: calibre of a gun; hence, metaph. size, weight, importance.

BOSKY: covered with underwood.

BOSOM: wish, heart's desire.

BOTS: worms which infest horses.

BOURN: a boundary. A brook.

BRACE: armour for the arm, state of defence.

BRACH: a hound bitch.

BRAID: deceitful.

BRAVE: handsome, well-dressed.

BRAVE: boast.

BRAVERY: finery. Boastfulness.

BRAWL: a kind of dance.

BREAST: voice.

BREATHE: to exercise.

BREECHING: liable to be whipped.

BREED-BATE: a fomenter of trouble or debate.

BREESE: the gadfly.

BRIBE-BUCK: a buck given away in presents.

BRING: to attend one on a journey.

BROCK: a badger.

BROKE: to act as a procurer.

BROKEN: having lost some teeth by age.

BROKEN MUSIC: the music of stringed instruments.

BROKER: an agent.

BROTHERHOOD: trading company.

BROWNIST: a sectary, a follower of Brown, the founder of the Independents.

BRUIT: noise, report, rumour.

BRUSH: rude assault.

BUCK: suds or lye for washing clothes in.

BUCK-BASKET: a soiled clothes basket.

BUCKING: washing.

BUCK-WASHING: washing in lye.

BUG: a bugbear, a spectre.

BULLY-ROOK: a bragging cheater.

BURGONET: a kind of helmet.

BURST: to break.

BUSKY: bushy.

BUTT-SHAFT: a light arrow for shooting at a target.

BUXOM: obedient.

BY'RLAKIN: by our little Lady: an oath.

CADDIS: worsted galloon, or trimming tape.

CADE: a cask or barrel.

CAGE: a prison.

CAIN-COLOURED: red (applied to hair).

CAITIFF: a captive, a slave; a mean fellow.

CALCULATE: prophesy.

CALIVER: a hand-gun.

CALLET: a trull.

CALLING: appellation.

CALM: qualm.

CAN: to know, be skilful in.

CANAKIN: a little can.

CANARY: a wine brought from the Canary Islands.

CANDLE-WASTERS: persons who sit up all night to drink.

CANKER: a caterpillar. The dog-rose.

CANSTICK: a candlestick.

CANTLE: a slice, corner.

CANTON: a canto.

CANVAS: to sift: hence, metaphorically, to prove.

CAPABLE: subject to. Intelligent. Capable of inheriting. Ample, capacious.

CAPITULATE: make a combined force.

CAPOCCHIA: a simpleton.

CAPRICIO: (Italian), caprice.

CAPRICIOUS: lascivious.

CAPTIOUS: capacious.

CARACK: a large ship of burden.

CARBONADO: meat scotched for broiling.

CARD: the diagram of points on a mariner's compass.

CAREIRE: the curvetting of a horse.

CARKANET: a necklace.

CARL: a churl, a husbandman.

CARLOT: a churl, a husbandman.

CASTILIAN: a native of Castile; used as a cant term.

CASTILIANO VULGO: a cant term, meaning, apparently, to use discreet language.

CATAIAN: a native of Cathay, Chinese.

CATLING: cat-gut.

CAUTEL: deceit.

CAUTELOUS: insidious.

CAVALERO: a cavalier, gentleman.

CAVIARE: the roe of sturgeon pickled; metaph. a delicacy not appreciated by the vulgar.

CEASE: decease.

CENSURE: judgment. To judge, criticise.

CEREMONY: a ceremonial rite or vestment.

CERTES: certainly.

CESS: rate, reckoning.

CHACE: a term at tennis.

CHAMBER: a species of great gun.

CHAMBERER: an effeminate man.

CHANSON: a song.

CHARACT: affected quality.

CHARACTER: handwriting. Write, engrave.

CHARACTERY: handwriting. That which is written.

CHARE: a turn of work, a chore.

CHARGE-HOUSE: a free-school.

CHARLES' WAIN: the Great Bear, the Plough.

CHARNECO: a species of sweet wine.

CHAUDRON: entrails.

CHEATER: for escheator, an officer who collected the fines to be paid into the Exchequer.

CHECK AT: in falconry, when a falcon foresakes her proper quarry for baser game.

CHEER: fortune, countenance.

CHERRY-PIT: a game played with cherrystones.

CHEVERIL: kid leather.

CHEWIT: a cough, a chatterer.

CHILDING: pregnant.

CH'ILL: vulgar for 'I will.'

CHIRURGEONLY: in a manner becoming a surgeon.

CHOPIN: a high shoe or clog.

CHRISTENDOM: the state of being a Christian.

CHRISTOM: clothed with a chrisom, the white garment put on newly-baptized children.

CHUCK: chicken, a term of endearment.

CHUFF: a coarse blunt clown.

CINQUE PACE: a kind of dance.

CIPHER: to decipher.

CIRCUMSTANCE: an argument.

CITAL: recital.

CITE: to incite.

CITTERN: a guitar.

CLACK-DISH: a beggar's dish.

CLAP I' THE CLOUT: to shoot an arrow into the bull's eye of the target.

160

CLAW: to flatter.
CLEPE: to call.
CLIFF: clef, the key in music.
CLING: to starve.
CLINQUANT: glittering.
CLIP: to embrace, enclose.
CLOUT: the mark in the middle of a target.
COAST: to advance, approach.
COBLOAF: a big loaf.
COCK: a cockboat.
COCK: a euphemism for God.
COCKLE: tares or darnel.
COCKNEY: a milksop.
COCK-SHUT-TIME: the twilight, when cocks and hens go to roost.
COG: to cheat, dissemble.
COGNIZANCE: badge, token.
COIGN: projecting corner stone.
COIL: tumult, turmoil.
COISTREL: a cowardly knave.
COLLECTION: drawing a conclusion.
COLLIED: blackened, clouded.
COLOUR: pretence.
COLOURABLE: specious, plausible.
COLT: to defraud, befool.
CO-MART: a joint bargain.
COMBINATE: betrothed.
COMMODITY: interest, profit.
COMMONTY: used ludicrously for comedy.
COMPACT: compacted, composed.
COMPETITOR: an associate, a partner.
COMPLEMENT: accomplishment.

COMPLEXION: humour.

COMPOSE: to agree.

COMPOSTION: composition, agreement.

COMPTIBLE: tractable.

CON: to learn by heart. To acknowledge.

CONCEIT: conception, opinion, fancy.

CONCUPY: concubine.

CONDITION: temper, quality.

CONDOLEMENT: grief.

CONFECT: to make up into sweetmeats.

CONFOUND: to consume, destroy.

CONJECT: conjecture.

CONSIGN: to sign a common bond, to confederate.

CONSORT: to accompany.

CONSTANCY: consistency, fidelity.

CONSTANT: settled, determined.

CONSTER: to construe.

CONTEMPTIBLE: contemptuous.

CONTINENT: that which contains.

CONTINUATE: uninterrupted.

CONTRACTION: the marriage contract.

CONTRARY: to oppose.

CONTRIVE: to spend (time).

CONTROL: to confute.

CONVENT: to convene, summon, to be convenient.

CONVERTITE: a convert.

CONVEY: to manage. To filch.

CONVINCE: to conquer, subdue.

CONVIVE: to feast together.

CONY-CATCH: to cheat, to dupe.

COOLING CARD: anything that dashes hopes.

COPATAIN HAT: a high-crowned hat.

COPE: to reward, to give in return.

COPPED: rising to a cop or head.

COPY: theme, example.

CORAGIO: (Italian) courage!

CORAM: an ignorant mistake for Quorum.

CORANTO: lively dance.

CORINTH: a cant term for a brothel.

CORINTHIAN: a wencher.

CORKY: dry like cork, withered.

CORNUTO: (Italian) a cuckold.

COROLLARY: surplus, additional.

CORPORAL: corporeal, bodily.

CORPORAL OF THE FIELD: an aide-de-camp.

CORRIVAL: rival.

COSTARD: the head.

COSTER-MONGER: peddling, mercenary.

COTE: a cottage.

COTE: to come alongside, overtake. To quote.

COT-QUEAN: an effeminate man, molly-coddle.

COUNT CONFECT: an affected nobleman.

COUNTENANCE: pretend; give support to.

COUNTERFEIT: portrait. A piece of base coin.

COUNTERPOINT: a counterpane.

COUNTERVAIL: to counterpoise, outweigh.

COUNTY: count, earl.

COUPLEMENT: union.

COURT HOLY-WATER: flattery.

COVENT: a convent.

COVER: to lay the table for dinner.

COWISH: cowardly.

COWL-STAFF: the staff for carrying a tub.

COX MY PASSION: an oath, for "God's Passion."

COY: to stroke, fondle. To show disdain.

COZEN: to cheat.

COZIER: a tailor or cobbler.

CRACK: to boast.

CRACK: a loud noise, clap. A forward boy.

CRACK-HEMP: a gallows-bird.

CRANK: a winding passage. To twist and turn.

CRANTS: garlands.

CRARE: a ship of burden.

CRAVEN: a dunghill cock, a coward.

CREATE: formed, compounded.

CREDENT: creditable. Credible. Credulous.

CRESCIVE: increasing.

CRESTLESS: not entitled to bear arms, lowborn.

CRISP: curled, winding.

CROSS: a coin stamped with a cross.

CROW-KEEPER: one who scares crows.

CROWNER: a coroner.

CROWNET: a coronet.

CRY: a pack of hounds or knaves.

CRY AIM: to encourage.

CUE: the last words of an actor's speech, the signal for the next actor to begin.

CUISSES: pieces of armour to cover the thighs.

CULLION: a base fellow.

CUNNING: skill, skilful.

CURB: to bend, truckle.

CURRENTS: occurrences.

CURST: shrewish, sharp tempered.

CURTAIL: a cur.

CURTAL: a docked horse.

CURTAL-AXE: a cutlass.

164

CUSTALORUM: a ludicrous mistake for Custos Rotulorum, a chief justice.

CUSTARD-COFFIN: the crust of a custard-pudding.

CUSTOMER: a common woman.

CUT: a cheat. 'To draw cuts' is to draw lots.

CYPRESS: a kind of crape.

DAFF: to befool. To put off.

DANGER: reach, control, power.

DANSKER: a Dane.

DARRAIGN: to set in array.

DAUB: to disguise.

DAUBERY: imposition, falsehood.

DEARN: hidden, solitary.

DEBOSHED: debauched, drunken.

DECK: to bedew, to adorn.

DECLINE: to enumerate.

DEEM: doom, judgment.

DEFEAT: to undo, destroy. Destruction.

DEFEATURE: disfigurement.

DEFENCE: art of fencing.

DEFEND: to forbid.

DEFY: renounce.

DEGREE: relative position or rank.

DEMERIT: merit, desert.

DENAY: denial.

DENIER: the 12th part of a French sou coin.

DENY: to refuse.

DEPEND: to be in service.

DEROGATE: degraded, debased.

DESCANT: comment on a given theme.

DETECT: to charge, blame.

DETERMINE: to conclude.

DICH: may it do.

DIFFUSED: confused.

DIGRESSION: transgression.

DIG-YOU-GOOD-DEN: give you good evening.

DILDO: the chorus or burden of a song.

DINT: stroke, impression.

DIRECTION: judgment, skill.

DISABLE: to disparage.

DISAPPOINTED: unprepared.

DISCASE: to undress.

DISCONTENT: a malcontent.

DISCOURSE: power of reasoning.

DISLIMN: to disfigure, transform, efface.

DISME: a tenth or tithe.

DISPARK: to destroy a park.

DISPONGE: to squeeze out as from a sponge.

DISPOSE: disposal, disposition. To arrange.

DISPOSITION: arrangement; behaviour.

DISPUTABLE: disputatious.

DISSEMBLY: used ridiculously for assembly.

DISTASTE: to offend the taste, disgust.

DISTEMPERED: discontented, disturbed.

DISTRACTION: a detached troop or company of soldiers.

DIVISION: a phrase or passage in a melody.

DOFF: to take off, remove. To put off with an excuse.

DOIT: a small Dutch coin, a trifle.

DOLE: portion dealt. Grief, lamentation.

DOTANT: one who dotes, a dotard.

DOUT: to quench.

DOWLAS: a kind of coarse sacking.

DOWLE: feather.

DOWN-GYVED: hanging down like gyves or fetters.

DRAB: a harlot.

DRAUGHT: a privy.

DRAWN: having his sword drawn.

DRIBBLING: falling wide of the mark.

DROLLERY: a puppet-show.

DRUMBLE: to dawdle.

DUC-DAME: duc-ad-me, bring him to me.

DUDGEON: hilt of a dagger.

DULL: soothing.

DUMP: sad tune.

DUP: lift up, undo.

EAGER: harsh, cutting, sour.

EANLING: a yeanling, a lamb.

EAR: to plough.

ECHE: to eke out.

ECSTACY: madness.

EFT: ready, convenient.

EISEL: vinegar.

ELD: old age.

EMBOSSED: swollen; foaming from exertion (of a hound).

EMBOWELLED: disembowelled.

EMBRASURE: embrace.

EMPERY: empire.

EMULATION: jealousy.

EMULOUS: jealous, ambitious.

ENCAVE: to place in a cave, to hide.

167

ENFEOFF: to hand over, surrender.

ENGINE: a machine of war.

ENGLUT: to swallow speedily.

ENGROSS: to make gross or fat.

ENGROSSMENT: immoderate acquisition.

ENKINDLE: to make keen.

ENMEW: to shut up, coop up.

ENSCONCE: to cover as with a fort; to take shelter.

ENSEAMED: fat, greasy.

ENSHIELD: guard, protect.

ENTERTAIN: take into service.

ENTERTAINMENT: treatment; reception.

ENTREATMENT: entreating.

EPHESIAN: a toper, a cant term.

EQUIPAGE: attendance, retinue.

EREWHILE: a short time since.

ESCOT: to pay a man's reckoning, to maintain.

ESPERANCE: hope, used as a war-cry.

ESPIAL: a scout or spy.

ESTIMATION: conjecture.

ESTRIDGE: ostrich.

EXCREMENT: outgrowths from the body like hair or nails.

EXECUTOR: an executioner.

EXEMPT: excluded, separated.

EXERCISE: a religious service.

EXHALE: to draw the sword.

EXHIBITION: allowance, pension.

EXIGENT: death, ending; emergency.

EXION: ridiculously used for 'action.'

EXPEDIENCE: purpose requiring haste.

EXPEDIENT: expeditious, swift.
EXPIATE: completed, fully arrived.
EXPOSTULATE: to expound, discuss.
EXPOSTURE: exposure.
EXPRESS: well made.
EXPULSE: to expel.
EXSUFFLICATE: contemptible, puffed out.
EXTEND: to seize, to magnify.
EXTERN: outward.
EXTIRP: to extirpate.
EXTRAUGHT: extracted, descended.
EXTRAVAGANT: foreign, wandering.
EYAS: a nestling hawk.
EYAS-MUSKET: a young sparrow-hawk, a sprightly
    boy.
EYE: a shade of colour, as in shot silk.
EYNE: eyes.

FACINOROUS: wicked.
FACT: guilt, crime.
FACTIOUS: instant, importunate.
FACULTY: essential virtue or power.
FADGE: to suit, turn out.
FADING: a kind of ending to a song.
FAIN: glad, gladly.
FAIR: beauty.
FAITOR: imposter, cheat.
FALLOW: fawn-coloured.
FALSING: deceptive.
FAMILIAR: a familiar spirit.
FANCY-FREE: untouched by love.
FANG: to seize.

FANTASTIC: a fantastical person.

FAP: drunk.

FARCED: stuffed out.

FARDEL: a burden.

FARTUOUS: used ridiculously for "virtuous."

FAT: hot; vat.

FAVOUR: countenance. Complexion. Quality.

FEAR: to frighten.

FEAT: dexterous, neat, becoming.

FEAT: to mirror, reflect.

FEATLY: nimbly, daintily.

FEATURE: beauty.

FEDERARY: confederate, accomplice.

FEEDER: agent, servant.

FEE-GRIEF: a private grief.

FEERE: a companion, spouse.

FEHEMENTLY: used ridiculously for "vehemently."

FELL: the hide.

FENCE: art or skill in defence.

FEODARY: one who holds an estate by suit or service to a superior lord; a dependant.

FESTINATELY: quickly.

FET: fetched.

FICO: a fig.

FIG: to insult.

FIGHTS: screens round a ship to conceal the men from the enemy.

FILE: to defile, pollute.

FILL-HORSE: shaft-horse.

FILLS: the shafts.

FINE: end.

FINELESS: endless.

170

FIRAGO: ridiculously used for 'Virago.'

FIRE-DRAKE: meteor;(slang) man with red nose.

FIRE-NEW: brand-new.

FIRK: to chastise.

FIT: a canto or division of a song. A trick or habit. A spasm.

FITCHEW: a polecat.

FIVES: a disease incident to horses.

FLAP-DRAGON: raisins in burning brandy.

FLAP-JACK: a pan-cake.

FLATNESS: depth.

FLAW: a gust of wind, or sudden emotion, fragment.

FLAW: to make a flaw in, to break.

FLECKED: spotted, streaked.

FLEET: to float. To pass away, to pass the time.

FLEETING: inconstant.

FLESHMENT: excitement arising from success.

FLEWED: with hanging chops, like hounds.

FLIGHT: archery contest.

FLIRT-GILL: a light woman.

FLOTE: wave, sea.

FLOURISH: ornament.

FLUSH: fresh, full of vigour, in full bloom.

FOIL: defeat, disadvantage.

FOIN: to fence, fight.

FOISON: plenty, abundance.

FOND: foolish, foolishly affectionate.

FOOT-CLOTH: a saddle-cloth hanging down to the ground.

FORBID: accursed, outlawed.

FORBODE: forbidden.

FORCE: to stuff, to cram.

FORDO: to kill, destroy. To weary.

FOREIGN: obliged to live abroad.

FOREPAST: former.

FORESLOW: to delay.

FORFEND: to forbid.

FORGETIVE: inventive.

FORKED: horned. Two-legged.

FORMAL: regular, normal.

FORSPEAK: to speak against.

FORSPENT: exhausted, weary.

FORTHRIGHT: a straight path.

FORWEARY: to weary, exhaust.

FOSSET-SELLER: seller of taps (faucets) for barrels.

FOX: a sword; a cant word.

FOX-SHIP: the cunning of the fox.

FRAMPOLD: peevish, disagreeable.

FRANK: the feeding place of swine, sty.

FRANKED: confined.

FRANKLIN: a freeholder, a small squire.

FRAUGHT: freight, the cargo of a ship.

FRAUGHTING: freight, the cargo of a ship.

FRESH: a spring of fresh water.

FRET: the stop of a musical instrument.

FRET: to wear away. To variegate, adorn.

FRIEND: to befriend.

FRIPPERY: an old-clothes shop.

FRONT: to affront, oppose.

FRONTIER: fortress.

FRONTLET: that which is worn on the forehead.

FRUSH: to break or bruise.

FRUSTRATE: frustrated.

FUB OFF: to put off.
FULFIL: to fill full.
FULLAM: a loaded die.
FULSOME: lustful, offensive.

GABERDINE: a loose outer coat, or smock frock.
GAD: a pointed instrument. Upon the gad, with impetuous haste, on the spur of the moment.
GAIN-GIVING: misgiving.
GALLIARD: a kind of dance.
GALLIASSE: a kind of ship.
GALLIMAUFRY: a ridiculous medley.
GALLOW: to scare.
GALLOWGLASS: the irregular infantry of Ireland, and the Highlands of Scotland.
GAMESTER: a frolicsome person. A loose woman.
GARBOIL: disorder, uproar.
GARNER: to lay by, as corn in a barn.
GAST: frightened.
GAUDY: festive.
GAZE: an object of wonder.
GEAR: matter of business of any kind.
GECK: a fool, butt.
GENERAL: the generality, the people.
GENEROSITY: noble birth.
GENEROUS: noble.
GENTILITY: good manners.
GENTLE: noble, well-born. To ennoble.
GENTRY: gentlemanly behaviour.
GERMAN: akin. Appropriate.
GERMEN: seed, embryo.
GEST: period; deed.

GIB: a he-cat.

GIFTS: talents, endowment.

GIGLOT: a wanton girl.

GILDER: a coin of the value of 1s. 6d. or 2s.

GIMMAL: double, jointed.

GIMMOR: contrivance.

GING: gang.

GLEEK: to scoff.

GLOSE: to comment; to intercept.

GLUT: to swallow.

GNARL: to snarl.

GOOD-DEED: indeed.

GOOD-DEN: good-evening.

GOOD-YEAR!: an oath (What the good year!)

GORBELLIED: corpulent.

GOURD: false dice.

GOUT: a drop.

GOVERNMENT: discretion, control.

GRACIOUS: abounding in grace.

GRAINED: engrained, dyed.

GRAMERCY: much thanks.

GRANGE: the farmstead attached to a monastery, a solitary farm-house.

GRATILLITY: a nonce-word: 'gratuity.'

GRATULATE: to congratulate.

GRAVE: to bury.

GREASILY: grossly.

GREEK: a bawd, buffoon.

GREENLY: foolishly.

GREET: to weep.

GRIZE: a step.

GROUNDLING: one who frequents the pit of a theatre.

GUARD: decoration, ornament.

GUARDAGE: guardianship.

GUINEA-HEN: a courtesan.

GULES: red, a term in heraldry.

GUN-STONE: a cannon ball.

GUST: taste, relish.

GYVE: to fetter.

HACK: to become common.

HAGGARD: a wild or unreclaimed hawk.

HAG-SEED: seed or offspring of a hag.

HAIR: grain, nature.

HALIDOM: holiness, used as an oath.

HALLOWMAS: All Hallows' Day.

HAP: chance, fortune.

HAPPILY: accidentally.

HANDSAW: perhaps a corruption of heronshaw; a heron.

HARDIMENT: defiance, brave deeds.

HARRY: to annoy, harass.

HAUGHT: haughty.

HAUNT: company.

HAVING: property, fortune.

HAVIOUR: behavior.

HAY: a term in fencing; a dance.

HEADY: violent, headlong.

HEBENON: henbane.

HEFT: a heaving.

HELM: to steer, manage.

HENCE: henceforward.

HENCHMAN: a page or attendant.

HENT: grasp, occasion for seizing.

HERMIT: a beadsman.

HEST: command, behest.

HIGHT: called.

HILD: pp. held.

HILDING: a paltry fellow.

HIREN: a prostitute, with a pun on the word "iron."

HOISE: to hoist, heave up on high.

HOIST: hoisted.

HOLP: helped.

HOME: to the utmost, fully.

HONEST: chaste, modest.

HONESTY: chastity.

HONEY-STALKS: red clover.

HOODMAN-BLIND: blindman's-buff.

HORN-MAD: furious, enraged.

HOROLOGE: a clock.

HOT-HOUSE: a brothel.

HOX: to hamstring.

HUGGER-MUGGER: secrecy.

HULL: to drift on the sea like a wrecked ship.

HUMOROUS: humid; full of humours.

HUNT-COUNTER: to follow the scent the wrong way.

HUNTS-UP: a hunting cry for daybreak.

HURLY: noise, confusion.

HURTLE: to clash noisily.

HUSBANDRY: frugality. Management.

HUSWIFE: a jilt.

ICE-BROOK: an icy-cold brook to temper steel.
I'FECKS: in faith, a euphemism.
IGNOMY: ignominy.
IMAGE: representation.
IMBARE: to bare, lay open.
IMMEDIACY: close connexion.
IMMOMENT: unimportant.
IMP: to graft, to splice a falcon's broken feathers.
IMP: a scion, a child.
IMPAWN: to stake, to risk.
IMPEACH: to bring into question. Impeachment.
IMPEACHMENT: cause of censure, hindrance.
IMPERCEIVERANT: undiscerning.
IMPETICOS: to pocket.
IMPORTANCE: importunity.
IMPORTANT: importunate.
IMPOSITION: command.
IMPRESE: a device with a motto.
IMPRESS: to compel to serve.
INCAPABLE: unconscious, unaware.
INCARNARDINE: to dye red.
INCENSED: incited, enraged.
INCH-MEAL: inch by inch.
INCLINING: inclination; compliant.
INCLIP: to embrace.
INCLUDE: conclude.
INCONY: fine, delicate.
INCORRECT: ill-regulated.
IND: India.
INDENT: to compound or bargain.
INDEX: a preface, contents.
INDIFFERENT: ordinary.

INDIGEST: shapeless mass.

INDITE: to invite. To convict.

INDUCTION: introduction, beginning.

INHABITABLE: uninhabitable.

INHERIT: to possess.

INHOOPED: penned up in hoops.

INKHORN-MATE: a contemptuous term for an ecclesiastic, or man of learning.

INKLE: a narrow fillet or tape.

INLAND: civilized, well-educated.

INLY: inwardly.

INSANE: that which causes insanity.

INSTANCE: example. Information. Reason, proof.

INTEND: to pretend.

INTENDMENT: intention.

INTENTIVELY: attentively.

INTERESSED: allied, interested.

INTRINSE: intricate.

INTRINSICATE: intricate.

INVENTION: imagination.

INWARD: an intimate friend; intimate.

INWARDNESS: intimacy.

IRREGULOUS: lawless, licentious.

JACK: a mean fellow.

JACK-A-LENT: a puppet thrown at in Lent.

JACK GUARDANT: a jack in office.

JADE: to whip, to treat with contempt.

JAR: the ticking of a clock.

JAUNCE: to cause a horse to prance; to trudge about.

JESS: a strap attached to the talons of a hawk.

JEST: to tilt in a tournament, to joust.
JET: to strut.
JOURNAL: daily.
JOVIAL: appertaining to Jove.
JUDICIOUS: critical.
JUMP: hazard.
JUMP: exactly, nicely.
JUT: to encroach.
JUTTY: jut out beyond; projection.
JUVENAL: youth, young man.

KAM: crooked, twisted.
KECKSY: hemlock-like weed.
KEECH: a lump of tallow.
KEEL: to skim, to cool.
KERN: the rude foot soldiers of the Irish.
KIBE: a chilblain.
KICKSHAWS: fancy trifles of food; frivolities.
KICKSY WICKSY: a wife, used in disdain.
KILN-HOLE: oven.
KINDLE: to bring forth young; used only of
    beasts.
KINDLESS: unnatural.
KINDLY: natural, generous.
KIRTLE: a gown.
KNAP: to snap, knock.
KNAVE: a boy. A serving-man.
KNOT: flower bed.

LABRAS: lips.
LACED-MUTTON: a courtezan.
LAG: the lowest of the people.

LAG: late, behindhand.

LAKIN: ladykin, little lady, "By'r lakin": an oath.

LAND-DAMN: a term of abuse.

LAPSED: taken, apprehended.

LARGE: licentious, free.

LARGESS: a present.

LASS-LORN: deserted by a mistress.

LATCH: to smear. To catch.

LATED: belated.

LATTEN: made of brass.

LAUND: lawn, clearing in a forest.

LAVOLTA: a dance.

LAY: wager.

LEAGUE: besieging army.

LEASING: lying.

LEATHER-COATS: russet apples.

LEECH: a physician.

LEER: countenance, complexion.

LEET: a manor court.

LEGE: to allege.

LEGERITY: lightness.

LEIGER: an ambassador resident abroad.

LEMAN: a lover or mistress.

LENTEN: meagre; appropriate to Lent.

L'ENVOY: the final stanza of a poem.

LET: hindrance; to hinder.

LETHE: death. A river in Hades.

LEVEL: to aim.

LEWD: ignorant, base.

LEWDSTER: a lewd person.

LIBBARD: a leopard.

LIBERAL: licentious.

LIBERTY: libertinism.

LIEF: dear. Willingly.

LIFTER: a thief.

LIGHT O' LOVE: a tune so called.

LIGHTLY: easily, generally.

LIKE: to liken, compare.

LIKE: likely.

LIKING: condition.

LIMBECK: an alembick, a still.

LIMBO: the abode of the just who died before Christ's coming; slang for prison.

LIME: to entangle as with bird-lime. To mix lime with beer or other liquor.

LIMN: to draw or paint.

LINE: support.

LINSTOCK: a staff with a match at the end used by gunners in firing cannon.

LIST: a strip of cloth: an enclosure for tilting.

LITHER: lazy.

LITTLE: miniature.

LIVELIHOOD: appearance of life.

LIVERY: legal proceedings to recover an inheritance.

LOB: a lout.

LOCKRAM: a sort of coarse linen.

LODE-STAR: the leading-star, pole-star.

LOGGATS: the game called nine-pins.

LOOF: to luff, bring a vessel up to the wind.

LOON: a low contemptible fellow.

LOTTERY: a prize.

LOUT: to treat one as a lout, with contempt.

LOZEL: a rascal.

LUBBER: a lout, a clumsy fellow.

LUCE: the pike or jack, a fresh-water fish.

LUNES: fits of lunacy.

LURCH: to outdo, to deprive of all chance.

LURE: a dummy bird to attract a hawk.

LUXURIOUS: lascivious.

LUXURY: lust.

LYM: a bloodhound.

MAGNIFICO: a Venetian nobleman.

MAGGOT-PIE: a magpie.

MAIL: cover as with a coat of mail.

MAIN-COURSE: the mainsail.

MAKE: to do up, bar.

MALKIN: a servant wench.

MALLECHO: mischief.

MAMMERING: hesitating.

MAMMET: a doll, a puppet.

MAMMOCK: tear to pieces.

MAN: to tame a hawk.

MANAGE: management, control of a horse.

MANDRAGORA or MANDRAKE: a plant of soporiferous quality, supposed to resemble a man.

MANKIND: having a masculine nature.

MARCHES: frontiers, borders.

MARCHPANE: a sweetmeat like marzipan.

MARGENT: margin.

MARRY: an exclamation of surprise, indignation, etc.

MARTLEMAS: Martinmas, 11th November, a word applied derisively to an old man.

MATCH: a compact, agreement.

182

MATE: to confound, dismay.

MEACOCK: tame, cowardly.

MEALED: mingled, stained.

MEAN: instrument used to promote an end; opportunity.

MEAN: the tenor part in a harmony.

MEASURE: traverse. A stately dance.

MEAZEL: a´leper.

MEDAL: a portrait in a locket.

MEDICINE: a physician.

MEED: reward, hire. Merit.

MEINY: retinue.

MELL: to mix, to meddle.

MEMORISE: to cause to be remembered.

MEPHISTOPHILUS: the name of a familiar spirit.

MERCATANTE: (Italian), a foreign trader.

MESS: a company of four.

METAPHYSICAL: supernatural.

METE-YARD: measuring-wand.

MEW UP: to confine.

MICHER: a truant.

MILL-SIXPENCE: a milled sixpence.

MINCING: affected.

MISCREATE: illegitimate, deformed.

MISERY: avarice.

MISPRISE: to despise. To mistake.

MISPRISION: mistaking, scorning.

MISSIVE: messenger.

MISTEMPERED: tempered for an evil purpose.

MISTHINK: to think ill of.

MISTRESS: the jack in bowling.

MOBLED: muffled, veiled.

MODERN: commonplace.

MODULE: a model, image.

MOIETY: a portion.

MOME: a stupid person.

MONTHS-MIND: a monthly commemoration of the dead, a strong desire.

MOON-CALF: a nick-name applied to Caliban.

MOONISH: inconstant.

MOP: grimace.

MORISCO: a morris-dancer.

MORRIS-PIKE: Moorish-pike.

MORT: death, applied to animals of the chase.

MORTIFIED: ascetic.

MOSE: applied to disease in a horse.

MOTION: a puppet-show.

MOTLEY: the many-coloured coat of a fool; one who plays the fool.

MOTLEY-MINDED: foolish.

MOUSE-HUNT: a weasel. A woman chaser.

MOW: to make grimaces.

MOY: the French "Moi", misinterpreted by Pistol as a coin.

MUCH: significant of contempt.

MUCH: used ironically.

MURE: a wall.

MUSS: a scramble, a children's game.

MUTINE: to mutiny; a mutineer.

NAPKIN: a handkerchief.

NAYWARD: towards denial, or unbelief.

NAYWORD: a catch-word, by-word.

NEB: beak, mouth.

184

NEELD: a needle.

NEIF: hand.

NEPHEW: a grandson, kinsman.

NETHER-STOCKS: stockings, the stocks.

NICK: score or reckoning.

NICK: to brand with folly.

NIGHTED: black as night.

NIGHT-RULE: nightly revel.

NINE MEN'S MORRIS: a game in which each side has nine pieces, "men"; the area in which it is played.

NINNY: a fool, a simpleton.

NOBLE: a coin, worth 6s. 8d.

NODDY: a dolt, simpleton.

NONCE: for the nonce, for the occasion.

NOOK-SHOTTEN: indented with bays and creeks.

NOURISH: nurse.

NOVUM: a game at dice.

NUTHOOK: a hook for pulling down nuts, a beadle.

O: a circle, the globe.

OAR: to row as with oars.

OBSEQUIOUS: a dutiful observance of funeral.

OBSTACLE: obstinate.

OCCUPATION: working men.

OCCURRENT: an incident.

OD'S: interj. euphemism for God's.

OD'S BODY: God's body.

OD'S PITTIKINS: God's pity.

OEILLIAD: an amorous glance.

O'ERPARTED: having too important a part to act.

185

OFFICE: function, service, office-holder.

OLD: slang; great, fine.

ONEYER: a banker. A doubtful word.

OPEN: to give tongue as a hound.

OPERANT: active.

OPPOSITE: adversary.

OPPOSITION: combat.

OR: before.

ORDINANCE: rank, order. That which is ordained.

ORGULOUS: proud.

ORT: leaving, refuse, fragment.

OSTENT: show, appearance.

OSTENTATION: show, appearance.

OUNCE: a beast of prey, a lynx.

OUPHE: a fairy, elf.

OUSEL-COCK: the blackbird.

OUT: in error, at variance.

OUT-LOOK: to face down, to outstare.

OUTWARD: outside, external appearance.

OWE: to own.

PACK: to plot, be in league.

PADDOCK: a toad.

PALABRAS: words, a cant term, from the Spanish.

PALE: an inclosure; to enclose.

PALL: to wrap as with a pall. To fail, be ruined.

PALMER: one who bears a palm-branch, in token of having made a pilgrimage to the Holy Land.

PALMY: flourishing.

PARCELLED: belonging to individuals.

186

PARD: the leopard.

PARITOR: an apparitor, summoner to a bishop's court.

PARLE: talk, parley.

PARLOUS: perilous. keen, shrewd.

PARTED: endowed, gifted.

PARTISAN: a pike.

PASH: the head.

PASH: to strike violently, to bruise, crush.

PASSANT: (of heraldic figures), walking.

PASSING: surpassingly, exceedingly.

PASSION: pain, compassion, grief.

PASSY-MEASURE: a stately dance, a pavane.

PASTRY: the room where pastry was made.

PATCH: a mean fellow, a clown.

PATCHERY: trickery.

PATH: to walk.

PATIENT: to make patient, to compose.

PATINE: the metal dish on which the bread is placed in the administration of the Eucharist.

PAUCA VERBA: few words.

PAUCAS: few, a cant word.

PAVIN: a dance, a pavane.

PAX: a small image of Christ.

PEAT: a term of endearment for a child.

PEDASCULE: a pedant, schoolmaster.

PEIZE: to balance, weigh down.

PELTING: paltry.

PERDU: lost. A sentry in a perilous post.

PERDURABLE: everlasting.

PERDY: a euphemism for Par Dieu.

PERFECT: certain, fully prepared.

PERIAPTS: charms worn round the neck.

PERJURE: a perjured person.

PERSPECTIVE: a telescope, or some sort of optical device.

PEW-FELLOW: a comrade.

PHEEZE: beat, chastise, settle.

PIA-MATER: the brain.

PICK: to pitch, throw.

PICKERS: (and stealers), the fingers, hands.

PICKT-HATCH: a place noted for brothels.

PIELED: shaven.

PILCHER: a scabbard. A pilchard.

PILL: to pillage.

PIN: a malady of the eye. The centre of a target.

PINFOLD: a pound, a place to confine lost cattle.

PIONED: meaning doubtful; perhaps trenched.

PLACKET: a petticoat-front. A woman.

PLAIN SONG: a simple air, the simple truth.

PLANCHED: made of boards.

PLANTATION: colonizing, planting a colony.

PLAUSIVE: plausible, acceptable.

PLEACHED: interwoven, folded.

POINT: a lace to hold up breeches.

POINT-DEVICE: derived from the French, faultless.

POISE: balance, weight, importance.

POLLED: shorn.

POMANDER: a perfumed ball.

POMEWATER: a kind of apple.

POOR-JOHN: salted fish.

POPINJAY: a parrot, a fop.

PORT: pomp, state, bearing. A gate.

PORTABLE: bearable.

PORTANCE: conduct, behavior.

POSSESS: to inform.

POTCH: to push violently, stab.

POTENT: a potentate.

POUNCET-BOX: a box for holding perfumes.

PRACTISE: wicked stratagem.

PRACTISANT: a confederate, conspirator.

PRANK: to dress up.

PRECEPT: a justice's summons, a warrant.

PREGNANT: fertile of invention. Ready. Obvious.

PRENOMINATE: to name beforehand, to prophesy.

PRE-ORDINANCE: old-established law.

PRESENCE: the presence-chamber. High bearing.

PREST: ready.

PRETENCE: design, plan.

PRETEND: to portend. To intend.

PREVENT: to anticipate.

PRICK: the mark denoting the hour on a dial.

PRICK: to incite. To mark off on a list.

PRICK-SONG: music sung in parts by note.

PRICKET: a stag of two years.

PRIG: thief.

PRIME: rank, lecherous.

PRIMERO: a game at cards.

PRINCIPALITY: one of the orders of angels.

PRINCOX: a coxcomb, forward fellow.

PRIZER: a prize-fighter.

PROCURE: to bring.

PROFACE: interj. may it do you good.

PROGRESS: a royal ceremonial journey.

PROJECT: to shape or contrive.

PROMPTURE: suggestion.

PRONE: ready, willing.

PROOF: strength of manhood.

PROPAGATE: to advance, to forward.

PROPAGATION: augmentation.

PROPER-FALSE: handsome deceiver.

PROPERTIED: endowed with the properties of. Treated as a property.

PROPOSE: To converse. To purpose.

PROROGUE: to defer.

PROVAND: provender.

PUCELLE: a virgin, the maid Joan of Arc.

PUDENCY: modesty.

PUGGING: thieving.

PUN: to pound.

PURCHASE: acquire, gain.

PUTTER-ON: an instigator.

PUTTER-OUT: one who lends money at interest.

PUTTOCK: a kite.

QUAIL: be afraid: to cause to quail. A loose woman.

QUAINT: curiously beautiful. Clever.

QUALIFY: to moderate.

QUALITY: Rank or condition. Natural gifts, skill.

QUARRY: game, a heap of game.

QUARTER: area assigned to a body of troops. Watch, guard.

QUAT: a pimple; used in contempt of a person.

QUEASY: squeamish, unsettled, ticklish.

QUELL: murder, slaughter.

190

QUENCH: to grow cool.
QUERN: a hand-mill.
QUEST: search, inquest, jury.
QUESTRIST: one who goes in search of another.
QUICK: living, pregnant, enlivening.
QUICKEN: to come to life.
QUIDDITY: subtlety, argument.
QUILLET: legal quibble.
QUINTAIN: a post for tilting at.
QUIP: sharp jest, a taunt.
QUIT: to requite, release, remit, pay back.
QUITTANCE: requital.
QUIVER: active, nimble.
QUOTE: to note, set down.

RABATO: a ruff, a collar.
RABBIT-SUCKER: a weasel, a baby rabbit.
RACE: breed; inherited nature, origin.
RACK: wreck, stretch, cause pain, misrepresent.
RACK: drifting cloud.
RAPTURE: a fit. Seizure, force of movement.
RASCAL: a lean deer.
RASH: quick, violent. To thrust in.
RATE: opinion, judgment, estimation.
RATE: to assign, to value. To scold.
RATOLORUM: corruption of Custos Rotulorum (Keeper of the Rolls).
RAUGHT: past tense of to reach.
RAVIN: ravenous. Devour.
RAWNESS: unprovided state, unprotected.
RAYED: arrayed, served, dirtied.
RAZED: slashed, cut ornamentally.

REBATE: to deprive of keenness.

REBECK: a three-stringed fiddle.

RECHEAT: to call back the hounds.

RECORD: to sing.

RECORDER: a flute.

RECURE: to cure, recover.

RED-LATTICE: suitable to an ale-house.

REDUCE: to bring back.

REECHY: smoky, dirty.

REFELL: to refute.

REFER: hand over, transfer.

REGIMENT: government.

REGREET: to salute, greet.

REGUERDON: requital, reward.

REMEMBER: to remind.

REMORSE: pity.

REMORSEFUL: full of pity, compassionate.

REMOTION: removal, remoteness.

REMOVED: remote, secluded.

RENDER: account, admission. To declare.

RENEGE: to renounce, to deny.

REPAIR: comfort. Resort, return.

REPEAL: to reverse the sentence of exile.

REPROOF: confutation.

REPUGN: to resist.

REQUIEM: mass for the dead.

RESOLVE: to satisfy. To dissolve.

RESPECT: consideration, comparison, esteem.

RESPECTIVE: respectful, thoughtful.

RETIRE: retreat, withdraw.

REVERB: to echo, reverberate.

REVOLT: a rebel.

RIB: to enclose as within ribs.
RIGGISH: wanton.
RIGOL: a circle.
RIPE: ready, mature.
RIVAGE: the shore.
RIVAL: a partner.
RIVALITY: equal rank.
RIVE: to fire, to split.
ROAD: a prostitute.
ROISTING: roistering, rousing.
ROMAGE: unusual stir, turmoil.
RONYON: a term of contempt used to a woman.
ROOD: the crucifix.
ROOK: a cheat.
ROPERY: roguery.
ROPE-TRICKS: trickery, roguery.
ROUND: to be with child.
ROUND: unceremonious.
ROUNDEL: a dance or song.
ROUNDURE: an enclosure; roundness.
ROUSE: carousal.
ROYNISH: mangy, scurvy.
RUBIOUS: ruddy, ruby-red.
RUDDOCK: the redbreast.
RUSH: a ring made of rushes.

SACRING-BELL: the little bell rung at mass to give
   notice that the elements are consecrated.
SAD: serious.
SAFE: sane, sound, secure.
SALT: lascivious, biting, tearful.
SANDED: sand coloured.

SANS: without.

SAUCY: lascivious.

SAW: a moral saying, a proverb.

SAY: assay, taste. Silken.

SCAFFOLDAGE: the gallery of a theatre.

SCALD: scurvy, scabby.

SCALE: to weigh in scales.

SCALL: a scab, a word of reproach.

SCAMBLE: to scramble.

SCAMEL: possibly sea-mel, or sea-mew.

SCAN: to examine carefully.

SCANT: to cut short, to spare; scanty.

SCANTLING: a small portion, sample.

SCAPE: to escape.

SCATHE: injury, injure.

SCATHFUL: destructive, harmful.

SCONCE: the head, protection, a fort.

SCOTCH: to bruise or cut slightly.

SCRIMER: a fencer.

SCROYLE: a scabby fellow, scoundrel.

SCULL: a shoal of fish.

SEAL: set one's seal to a deed; confirm. A token.

SEAM: fat.

SEAMY: showing the seam, the worst side.

SEAR: scorched, withered. To dry up.

SEARCH: to probe (a wound).

SECT: a cutting or scion. A political party.

SEEL: to sew up the eyes, to blind.

SEEMING: outward manner and appearance.

SEEN: versed, instructed.

SELD: seldom.

SELF-BOUNTY: native goodness.
SEMBLABLY: alike.
SENIORY: seniority.
SENNET: a flourish of trumpets.
SEPULCHRE: to bury.
SEQUESTRATION: separation.
SERE: dry, withered.
SERJEANT: a bailiff.
SERPICO: a skin disease.
SERVICEABLE: diligent in service.
SETEBOS: a fiend feared by Caliban.
SETTER: a spy for thieves.
SEVERAL: privately owned land; enclosed pasture.
SHARDS: shreds, broken fragments of pottery.
SHARDS: the wing cases of beetles.
SHARKED: snatched up, collected hastily.
SHEER: pure. Unmixed.
SHENT: rebuked, blamed. Hurt.
SHERIFF'S-POST: a post at the door of a sheriff, to which royal proclamations were fixed.
SHIVE: slice.
SHOT: the reckoning at an ale-house.
SHOUGHS: shaggy dogs.
SHOVEL-BOARD: game played by sliding metal pieces along a board at a mark.
SHREWD: mischievous, shrewish.
SHRIFT: confession. Absolution.
SHRIVE: to hear or make confession.
SHROUD: protect, cover, hide.
SIEGE: seat. Stool. Rank.
SIGHT: an aperture in a helmet. A visor.
SIGHTLESS: invisible. Unsightly.

SILLY: simple, rustic.

SIMULAR: counterfeit, feigned. A simulator.

SINGLE: feeble.

SIR: a title often applied to a bachelor of arts and priests as well as to knights.

SITH: since.

SITHENCE: since.

SIZES: allowances.

SKAINS-MATES: scapegraces.

SKILL: to be of importance, to matter.

SKIMBLE-SKAMBLE: rambling, disjointed.

SKINKER: a drawer of liquor.

SKIRR: to scour.

SLAVE: to enslave.

SLEAVE: skein of silk.

SLEDDED: sledged.

SLEIDED: untwisted, raw, applied to silk.

SLIP: a counterfeit coin.

SLIPPER: slippery.

SLIVER: split, tear off. A branch.

SLOPS: loose breeches.

SLUBBER: to perform hurriedly. To smear.

SMOOTH: to flatter.

SNEAP: rebuke, snub, pinch.

SNECK-UP: go hang!

SNUFF: anger. 'Take in snuff', take offence.

SOFTLY: gently.

SOIL: spot, tarnish.

SOLICIT: solicitation.

SOLIDARE: a small coin.

SOMETIMES: formerly, former.

SOOTH: truth. Conciliation.

SOREL: a buck of the third year.

SORRY: sorrowful, dismal.

SORT: a company. Rank, condition. Lot. 'In a sort,' in a manner.

SORT: to choose. to suit. To consort. To ordain.

SOT: fool, drunkard.

SOUL-FEARING: terrifying.

SOWL: to lug, drag.

SOWTER: name of a dog.

SPED: settled, done for.

SPEED: fortune.

SPERR: to bolt, fasten.

SPIAL: spy.

SPILL: to destroy.

SPILTH: spilling.

SPLEEN: violent feeling; anger, irritability, laughter.

SPRAG: quick.

SPRINGHALT: stringhalt, a disease of horses.

SPRITED: haunted.

SPURS: roots of trees.

SQUARE: to quarrel, measure.

SQUARE: the front part of a woman's dress.

SQUARE: fair, straightforward.

SQUARER: quarreller, swaggerer.

SQUASH: an unripe peascod.

SQUIER: a square or rule.

SQUINY: to squint.

STAGGERS: a disease in horses, attended with giddiness.

STAIN: to disfigure, tarnish.

STALE: a decoy. A gull. A prostitute.

STALE: urine.

STANIEL: an inferior kind of hawk.

STATE: a canopied chair.

STATION: attitude, stance.

STATIST: a statesman.

STATUTE-CAPS: woollen caps worn by citizens.

STEAD: to help, to act instead.

STEELED: set or fixed, delineated.

STERNAGE: steerage, course.

STICKLER: an arbitrator in combats.

STIGMATIC: branded by deformity.

STILL: constant.

STILLY: softly, silently.

STINT: to stop, to check.

STITHY: a smith's forge. To forge.

STOCCADO: a stoccata, or thrust in fencing.

STOCK: thrust.

STOMACH: courage. Appetite, inclination.

STONE-BOW: a cross-bow for throwing stones.

STOUP: a cup, flagon.

STOVER: fodder.

STRAIGHT: immediately.

STRAIN: lineage. Disposition. To embrace.

STRANGE: foreign. Coy, reserved. Marvellous.

STRANGENESS: coyness, reserve.

STRANGER: foreigner.

STRAPPADO: a kind of punishment.

STRICTURE: strictness.

STROSSERS: trousers.

STUCK: a sword-thrust (from stoccata).

STY: to lodge as in a sty.

SUBSCRIBE: to yield, succumb, write down.

SUCCESS: issue, consequence. Succession.

SUDDEN: hasty, rash.
SUFFERANCE: suffering, forbearance.
SUGGEST: to tempt, entice, persuade.
SUGGESTION: temptation, incitement.
SUITED: dressed.
SULLEN: doleful, melancholy.
SUMPTER: a pack-horse, drudge.
SUPPOSE: supposition, substitution.
SUPPOSED: counterfeit.
SURCEASE: cessation, death.
SURPRISE: to capture by surprise.
SUR-REINED: over-worked.
SUSPECT: suspicion.
SUSPIRE: to breathe.
SWABBER: a sweeper of the deck of a ship.
SWARTH: black.
SWARTH: quantity of grass cut down by one sweep of the scythe.
SWASHER: swaggerer.
SWATH: The same as 'swarth.'
SWATHLING: swaddling.
SWAY: to move on, advance.
SWIFT: ready, quick.
SWINGE-BUCKLER: a bully, a swashbuckler.

TABLE: a tablet, note-book, painting surface.
TABLES: the game of backgammon. A note-book.
TABOR: a small side-drum.
TABOURINE: tambourine, drum.
TAG: the rabble.
TAINT: stain, defile; be infected by.
TAINTURE: defilement.

TAKE: to infect, bewitch.

TAKE OUT: to copy.

TAKE UP: to borrow money, or buy on credit. To make up a quarrel.

TAKING: infection, malignant influence.

TAKING OFF: murder.

TALE: counting, reckoning.

TALL: strong, valiant.

TALLOW-CATCH: a lump of tallow.

TANG: twang, sound.

TANLING: anything tanned by the sun.

TARRE: to excite, urge on.

TARRIANCE: delay.

TARTAR: Tartarus, hell.

TASK: to employ. Challenge.

TASKING: challenging.

TASTE: enjoy sexually.

TAWDRY-LACE: a rustic necklace.

TAXATION: satire, sarcasm. Demand.

TAXING: satire, censure.

TEEN: grief.

TELL: to count.

TEMPER: to mix, to soften.

TEMPERANCE: temperature.

TEND: to attend to.

TENDER: offer, desire, esteem. To have consideration for.

TENT: to probe as a wound.

TERCEL: the male of the goshawk.

TERMAGANT: a ranting character in old plays.

TESTED: pure, assayed.

TESTERN: to reward with a tester, or six-pence.

THARBOROUGH: (corrupted from 'third-borough') a constable.

THEORICK: theory.

THEWS: sinews, muscles.

THICK: (of speech) huskily.

THICK-PLEACHED: thickly intertwined.

THIRD-BOROUGH: a constable.

THOUGHT: anxiety, grief.

THRASONICAL: boastful.

THREE-MAN BEETLE: a wooden mallet worked by three men.

THREE-MAN-SONG-MEN: singers of glees in three parts.

THREE-PILE: three-piled velvet.

THRENE: lament.

THRID: thread, fibre.

THROE: to put in agonies, cause pain.

THRUM: the tufted end of a thread in weaving.

THRUMMED: made of coarse ends or tufts.

TICKLE: ticklish.

TIGHT: nimble, active. Water-tight.

TIKE: a cur.

TILLY-VALLY: an exclamation of contempt.

TILTH: tillage.

TIMELESS: untimely.

TINCT: stain, dye.Colour of the elixir of life.

TIRE: attire, head-dress.

TIRE: to tear as a bird of prey. Devour.

TIRE: attire, headdress.

TOD: a tod of wool (28lbs).

TOKENED: marked with plague spots.

TOKENS: plague spots; marks of infection.

TOLL: to exact toll. To pay toll.

TOPLESS: supreme, without superior.

TOUCH: touchstone. Trait. An acute feeling.

TOUCHED: pricked, infected.

TOUSE: to pull, tear.

TOWARD: nearly ready, impending.

TOYS: trifles, foolish tricks.

TRADE: beaten path.

TRAJECT: a ferry.

TRANSLATED: transformed.

TRASH: to check, as a huntsman his hounds.

TRAY-TRIP: an old game played with dice.

TREACHERS: traitors, deceivers.

TREATIES: entreaties.

TRENCHED: carved, engraved.

TRICK: fashion. Distinguishing characteristic. Knack.

TRICK: to dress up.

TRICKED: blazoned, spotted.

TRICKING: ornament, costumes.

TRICKSY: elegantly.

TRIPLE: third.

TROJAN: a cant word for a thief.

TROLL-MY-DAMES: (Fr. *trou-madame*;) a game like bagatelle.

TROTH-PLIGHT: betrothed.

TROW: to trust, think.

TRUE: honest.

TRUNDLE-TAIL: a long-tailed dog.

TUCKET-SONANCE: a flourish on the trumpet.

TUNDISH: a funnel.

TURLYGOOD: bedlam-beggars, gypsies.

202

TWIGGEN: made of twigs, wicker.

TWILLED: Retained by woven branches.

TWINK: a twinkling.

TWIRE: to peep.

UMBERED: stained, dark, as with umber.

UNANELED: without extreme unction.

UNAVOIDED: unavoidable.

UNBARBED: uncovered, bare.

UNBATED: unblunted.

UNBOLT: to disclose, explain.

UNBOLTED: unsifted, unrefined.

UNBREATHED: unpractised.

UNCAPE: to throw off the hounds.

UNCHARGED: undefended, acquitted.

UNCLEW: to unravel, undo.

UNCOINED: unalloyed, unfeigned.

UNDERGO: to undertake.

UNDERTAKER: one who takes up another's quarrel.

UNDER-WROUGHT: undermined.

UNEATH: hardly.

UNEXPRESSIVE: inexpressible, beyond praise.

UNFAIR: to deprive of beauty.

UNHATCHED: undisclosed.

UNHOUSELED: without receiving the sacrament.

UNIMPROVED: undisciplined, inexperienced.

UNION: a pearl.

UNKIND: unnatural.

UNLIVED: bereft of life.

UNMANNED: untamed, applied to a hawk.

UNOWED: unowned.

UNPREGNANT: unready to act.

UNPROPER: common to all, not one's own.

UNQUESTIONABLE: averse to questioning.

UNREADY: undressed.

UNRESPECTIVE: inconsiderate. Undiscriminating.

UNSISTING: unresisting.

UNSTANCHED: incontinent.

UNTEMPERING: unsoftening.

UNTENTED: unsearchable, incurable.

UNTRADED: unused, uncommon.

UNVALUED: priceless. Of little value.

UPSPRING REEL: a boisterous dance.

URCHIN: the hedge-hog.

USANCE: usury.

USE: interest, custom, trust.

UTIS: merriment which accompanied a festival.

UTTER: to expel, put forth, sell.

UTTERANCE: extremity, the bitter end.

VADE: to fade.

VAIL: to lower, submit. Sinking.

VALANCED: fringed (with a beard).

VALIDITY: value, worth.

VANTAGE: advantage.

VANTBRACE: armour for the forearm.

VARLET: a servant, valet. A rascal.

VAST: waste, desert.

VASTIDITY: immensity.

VASTY: vast, immense.

VAUNT: the van, the beginning.

VAUNT-COURIERS: forerunners.

VAWARD: the van, vanguard, advanced guard.

VEGETIVES: herbs, vegetables.

VELURE: velvet.

VELVET-GUARDS: velvet trimmings; applied metaphorically to the citizens who wore them.

VENEW: a bout in fencing, a term applied to repartee and sallies of wit.

VENGE: to avenge.

VENTAGES: holes in a flute or flageolet.

VERY: true, real.

VIA: away!

VICE: the buffoon in the old morality plays.

VIE: to challenge a term at cards. To compete.

VIEWLESS: invisible.

VILLAIN: a lowborn man: a scoundrel.

VINEWED: mouldy.

VIOL-DE-GAMBOYS: a bass viol.

VIRGINALLING: playing with the fingers, as on the virginals.

VIRTUE: the essential excellence. Valour.

VIRTUOUS: excellent, potent.

VIZAMENT: advisement, counsel.

VOLUBLE: fickle.

VOTARIST: votary, one who has taken a vow.

VULGAR: the common people.

VULGARLY: publicly.

WAFT: to wave, beckon. To turn, carry by sea.

WAFTAGE: passage by water.

WAFTURE: waving, beckoning.

WAGE: to reward as with wages.

WAILFUL: lamentable.

WAIST: the middle of a ship.

WANNION: 'With a wannion' — 'with a vengeance.'

WAPPENED: withered, overworn.

WARD: guard. Prison. Safety.

WARDEN: a large pear used for baking.

WARDER: truncheon, staff.

WARN: to summon.

WASSAIL: a drinking bout. Festivity.

WAT: a familiar word for a hare.

WATCH: a watch light. Wakefulness.

WATCH: to tame by keeping constantly awake.

WATER-GALL: a secondary rainbow.

WATER-RUG: a kind of dog.

WATER-WORK: painting in distemper or water colour.

WAX: to grow.

WEATHER-FEND: defend from the weather, shelter.

WEB AND PIN: the cataract in the eye.

WEE: to think.

WEED: garment.

WEET: to know.

WELKIN: the sky; sky-blue.

WELL-LIKING: in good condition, plump.

WEND: to go.

WESAND: the wind-pipe.

WHELK: a weal, pimple.

WHELKED: marked with whelks or protuberances.

WHEN: an exclamation of impatience.

WHIFFLER: an officer who clears the way in processions.

WHILE-ERE: a little while ago.

WHILES: until.

206

WHIP-STOCK: handle of a whip.

WHIST: hushed, silent.

WHITE: the centre of an archery butt.

WHITELY: pale-faced.

WHITING-TIME: bleaching time.

WHITSTER: bleacher.

WHITTLE: a clasp knife.

WHOO-BUB: hubbub.

WIDOW: to endow with a widow's right.

WIDOWHOOD: widow's jointure.

WIGHT: person.

WILDERNESS: wildness.

WIMPLED: veiled, hooded, blindfolded.

WINDOW-BARS: lattice-work across a woman's stomacher.

WINDRING: winding.

WINTER-GROUND: to protect (a plant) from frost.

WIS: in the compound 'I wis,' certainly.

WISTLY: wistfully.

WIT: knowledge, wisdom.

WITHOUT: beyond.

WITS: five, the five senses.

WITTOL: a contented cuckold.

WITTY: intelligent.

WOMAN-TIRED: hen-pecked.

WONDERED: marvellously gifted.

WOOD: mad.

WOODCOCK: a simpleton.

WOODMAN: a hunter; so, of women.

WOOLWARD: shirtless.

WORD: flatter or put off with words. The Bible.

WORLD: 'To go to the world', to get married; 'a

woman of the world', a married woman.

WORM: a serpent.

WORTS: cabbages.

WOT: to know.

WOUND: twisted about.

WREAK: vengeance. To avenge.

WREAKFUL: revengeful, avenging.

WREST: an instrument for tuning a harp. To devise, pervert.

WRIT: gospel, truth. Document.

WRITHLED: shrivelled, wrinkled.

WROTH: misfortune.

WRUNG: twisted, strained.

WRY: to swerve, to go astray.

YARE: ready, swift, easily handled.

YARELY: readily, nimbly.

Y-CLAD: clad.

Y-CLEPED: called, named.

YEARN: to grieve, vex.

YELLOWNESS: jealousy.

YELLOWS: a disease of horses.

YEOMAN: a sheriff's officer. A freeholder or farmer.

YIELD: to reward. To report.

YOND: yonder.

ZANY: a clown, gull. A fool's stooge.

Other titles in the
Charnwood Library Series:

PAY ANY PRICE
Ted Allbeury

After the Kennedy killings the heat was on — on the Mafia, the KGB, the Cubans, and the FBI . . .

MY SWEET AUDRINA
Virginia Andrews

She wanted to be loved as much as the first Audrina, the sister who was perfect and beautiful — and dead.

PRIDE AND PREJUDICE
Jane Austen

Mr. Bennet's five eligible daughters will never inherit their father's money. The family fortunes are destined to pass to a cousin. Should one of the daughters marry him?

THE GLASS BLOWERS
Daphne Du Maurier

A novel about the author's forebears, the Bussons, which gives an unusual glimpse of the events that led up to the French Revolution, and of the Revolution itself.

CHINESE ALICE
Pat Barr

The story of Alice Greenwood gives a complete picture of late 19th century China.

UNCUT JADE
Pat Barr

In this sequel to CHINESE ALICE, Alice Greenwood finds herself widowed and alone in a turbulent China.

THE GRAND BABYLON HOTEL
Arnold Bennett

A romantic thriller set in an exclusive London Hotel at the turn of the century.

SINGING SPEARS
E. V. Thompson

Daniel Retallick, son of Josh and Miriam (from CHASE THE WIND) was growing up to manhood. This novel portrays his prime in Central Africa.

A HERITAGE OF SHADOWS
Madeleine Brent

This romantic novel, set in the 1890's, follows the fortunes of eighteen-year-old Hannah McLeod.

BARRINGTON'S WOMEN
Steven Cade

In order to prevent Norway's gold reserves falling into German hands in 1940, Charles Barrington was forced to hide them in Borgas, a remote mountain village.

THE PLAGUE
Albert Camus

The plague in question afflicted Oran in the 1940's.

THE RESTLESS SEA
E. V. Thompson

A tale of love and adventure set against a panorama of Cornwall in the early 1800's.

THE RIDDLE OF THE SANDS
Erskine Childers

First published in 1903 this thriller, deals with the discovery of a threatened invasion of England by a Continental power.

WHERE ARE THE CHILDREN?
Mary Higgins Clark

A novel of suspense set in peaceful Cape Cod.

KING RAT
James Clavell

Set in Changi, the most notorious Japanese POW camp in Asia.

THE BLACK VELVET GOWN
Catherine Cookson

There would be times when Riah Millican would regret that her late miner husband had learned to read and then shared his knowledge with his family.

THE WHIP
Catherine Cookson

Emma Molinero's dying father, a circus performer, sends her to live with an unknown English grandmother on a farm in Victorian Durham and to a life of misery.

SHANNON'S WAY
A. J. Cronin

Robert Shannon, a devoted scientist had no time for anything outside his laboratory. But Jean Law had other plans for him.

THE JADE ALLIANCE
Elizabeth Darrell

The story opens in 1905 in St. Petersburg with the Brusilov family swept up in the chaos of revolution.

THE DREAM TRADERS
E. V. Thompson

This saga, is set against the background of intrigue, greed and misery surrounding the Chinese opium trade in the late 1830s.

BERLIN GAME
Len Deighton

Bernard Samson had been behind a desk in Whitehall for five years when his bosses decided that he was the right man to slip into East Berlin.

HARD TIMES
Charles Dickens

Conveys with realism the repulsive aspect of a Lancashire manufacturing town during the 1850s.

THE RICE DRAGON
Emma Drummond

The story of Rupert Torrington and his bride Harriet, against a background of Hong Kong and Canton during the 1850s.

FIREFOX DOWN
Craig Thomas

The stolen Firefox — Russia's most advanced and deadly aircraft is crippled, but Gant is determined not to abandon it.

THE DOGS OF WAR
Frederic Forsyth

The discovery of the existence of a mountain of platinum in a remote African republic causes Sir James Manson to hire an army of trained mercenaries to topple the government of Zangaro.

THE DAYS OF WINTER
Cynthia Freeman

The story of a family caught between two world wars — a saga of pride and regret, of tears and joy.

REGENESIS
Alexander Fullerton

It's 1990. The crew of the US submarine ARKANSAS appear to be the only survivors of a nuclear holocaust.

SEA LEOPARD
Craig Thomas

HMS 'Proteus', the latest British nuclear submarine, is lured to a sinister rendezvous in the Barents Sea.

THE TORCH BEARERS
Alexander Fullerton

1942: Captain Nicholas Everard has to escort a big, slow convoy . . . a sacrificial convoy.

DAUGHTER OF THE HOUSE
Catherine Gaskin

An account of the destroying impact of love which is set among the tidal creeks and scattered cottages of the Essex Marshes.

FAMILY AFFAIRS
Catherine Gaskin

Born in Ireland in the Great Depression, the illegitimate daughter of a servant, Kelly Anderson's birthright was poverty and shame.

THE EXPLORERS
Vivian Stuart

The fourth novel in 'The Australians' series which continues the story of Australia from 1809 to 1813.

IN HIGH PLACES
Arthur Hailey

The theme of this novel is a projected Act of Union between Canada and the United States in order that both should survive the effect of a possible nuclear war.

RED DRAGON
Thomas Harris

A ritual murderer is on the loose. Only one man can get inside that twisted mind — forensic expert, Will Graham.

CATCH-22
Joseph Heller

Anti-war novels are legion; this is a war novel that is anti-death, a comic savage tribute to those who aren't interested in dying.

THE ADVENTURERS
Vivian Stuart

The fifth in 'The Australians' series, opens in 1815 when two of its principal characters take part in the Battle of Waterloo.

THE FOUNDER OF THE HOUSE
Naomi Jacob

The first volume of a family saga which begins in Vienna, and introduces Emmanuel Gollantz.

"THAT WILD LIE . . . "
Naomi Jacob

The second volume in the Gollantz saga begun with THE FOUNDER OF THE HOUSE.

IN A FAR COUNTRY
Adam Kennedy

Christine Wheatley knows she is going to marry Fred Deets, that is until she meets Roy Lavidge.

ONCE IN A LIFETIME
Danielle Steel

To the doctors the woman in the ambulance was just another casualty — more beautiful than most . . .